# To Hell's Mouth and Back

## Pilgrimage, suffering and hope

Trystan Owain Hughes

**BRF**
Ministries

**BRF** Ministries

15 The Chambers, Vineyard
Abingdon OX14 3FE
**+44 (0)1865 319700 | brf.org.uk**

Bible Reading Fellowship is a charity (233280)
and company limited by guarantee (301324),
registered in England and Wales

EU Authorised Representative: Easy Access System Europe – Mustamäe tee 50,
10621 Tallinn, Estonia, **gpsr.requests@easproject.com**

ISBN 978 1 80039 426 1
First published 2025
All rights reserved

**Acknowledgements**
Unless otherwise stated, scripture quotations are taken from The Holy Bible, New
International Version (Anglicised edition) copyright © 1979, 1984, 2011 by Biblica.
Used by permission of Hodder & Stoughton Publishers, an Hachette UK company.
All rights reserved. 'NIV' is a registered trademark of Biblica. UK trademark number
1448790.

Scripture quotations marked RSV are taken from The Revised Standard Version
of the Bible, copyright © 1946, 1952, 1971 by the Division of Christian Education
of the National Council of the Churches of Christ in the United States of America.
Used by permission. All rights reserved.

Scripture quotations marked NKJV are taken from the New King James Version®.
Copyright © 1982 by Thomas Nelson. Used by permission. All rights reserved.

Every effort has been made to trace and contact copyright owners for material
used in this resource. We apologise for any inadvertent omissions or errors, and
would ask those concerned to contact us so that full acknowledgement can be
made in the future.

A catalogue record for this book is available from the British Library

'Weaving together his experience of walking an ancient pilgrim's way in his beloved North Wales and his experience of serious injury, Trystan Owain Hughes describes in this compelling book how we can learn to see God at work in our lives, even in the darkest of times. Through vivid narrative and honest reflection, peppered with references to poetry and novels as well as scripture, he draws us to reflect on our own journeys and pilgrimages, both seen and unseen. With questions for reflection at the end of each chapter, this is a wonderful and enriching book for both individuals and study groups to engage with.'
**Cherry Vann, Archbishop of Wales**

'In this moving and beautifully paced book, we are invited to share different kinds of pilgrimage – not only pilgrimage to holy places, but the journey into the pervasive divine presence and gift in the world, and the journey into what it is to live as a vulnerable and suffering body. God is the magnetic centre for all these journeys. This is a wonderful book of reflection, lament and celebration.'
**Rowan Williams, theologian and former Archbishop of Canterbury**

'Not just a story of a walk, but of a life. Trystan's book is poignant, challenging and excruciatingly honest. It reminds us that hope can outshine the deepest despair.'
**Rob Parsons, OBE, author and speaker**

'Through telling the story of his own journeying, Trystan Owain Hughes has produced a doggedly honest, deeply insightful, and rich spiritual resource for our own journeys through this life. The book takes the Welsh landscape, beautiful and terrible in equal measure, and uses it to draw a landscape of the human soul, providing prayerful and practical landmarks to remind us that it is Christ's landscape and he journeys with us.'
**Joanna Collicutt, Karl Jaspers lecturer in psychology and spirituality at Ripon College, Cuddesdon**

'This invitation to join Trystan Owain Hughes on the Pilgrim's Way is a powerful window into the gift and depth of pilgrimage. The combination of his vulnerability and attentiveness to wisdom, from St Augustine to Depeche Mode, make him a life-giving theologian and a hopeful human being. I will certainly return to this book.'
**Paul Davies, Bishop of Dorking**

'A powerful, beautifully written evocation of two "pilgrimages": the first undertaken by choice, along the pilgrim pathways of Wales; the second imposed by circumstances, as pain comes to dominate the writer's life. His searing honesty encourages us to discover hope in the midst of struggle and share his hard-won realisation that "opening ourselves to God's light and love can transform all our journeys".'
**Dee Dyas, director of the Centre for Pilgrimage Studies, University of York**

'This is a powerful and moving book, honest and unflinching in its depiction of the author's experience of two types of "pilgrimage". Exploring outwards from his personal journeys, Trystan draws on his own wisdom and that of many others to encourage deeper reflection on the challenges and rewards of pilgrimage.'
**Sally Welch, writer and pilgrim**

'This is a beautiful book in which Trystan Owain Hughes uses a well-trodden pilgrim path to explore with tenderness and honesty the deep and unanswerable questions of suffering. The insights he gains from this journey of the soul are both comforting and challenging, but above all reveal the precious and robust hope that is at the heart of Christ's kingdom.'
**Michael Mitton, writer, speaker, spiritual director**

'Gentle and profound, this book is a must-read for all who are mired in suffering.'
**Tanya Marlow, author and campaigner**

# Contents

# Acknowledgements

I wish to extend my deepest gratitude to the friends and family who have supported my writing over the years. Your endless enthusiasm and love have transformed the arduous process of writing into a truly rewarding adventure. This book stands as one of my most personal works, and I remain profoundly thankful for every bit of encouragement along the way.

A very special thank you goes to Sue Hurrell (and Bruce) and my wife Sandra, whose wise suggestions and painstaking chapter-by-chapter proofreading have enriched this work beyond measure. I am also hugely grateful to Peter Jones, Gwynan Hughes, Ainsley Griffiths, Jenny Wigley, Gaz Roberts, Wynford Ellis Owen and Eleanor Williams for their invaluable advice and assistance. Many thanks as well to everyone at BRF Ministries for believing my writing is worth sharing with others.

This book is dedicated, though, to those who journeyed with me on my two pilgrimages. Their company, support and compassion lifted and sustained me every step of the way.

**Pilgrimage One (Pilgrim's Way, North Wales)**
Thanks to Mum and Dad (Ros and Berw), Sandra Hughes, Angharad Sherrington, Perry Buck, Dafydd Bathers, George Oliver, Meinir Pierce Jones, Denise and Geoff Templeton, and Robin Fox.

**Pilgrimage Two (The red sofa, Roath Park, Cardiff)**
Thanks to Colin and Ann Francis, Haydn and Jill Hopkins, Chris Burr, Andy Wilkinson and Helen Blakely, Gwilym Roberts, Wyn Griffith, Gareth Erlandson, Jenny Wigley, Linda Alexandra, Anneliese Harnisch, Siôn Brynach, Julie and Martin Davies, Greg Dixon, Kath and Mike Lawley, Paul Fitzpatrick, Steve Edwards, Andrew James, Natalie Garrett, Emil

Evans, Gareth Harcombe, Jordan Hillebert, Caroline Downs, Richard Lowndes, Paul Francis, Norman Adams, Archbishop Barry Morgan, and to the wonderful church community of Christ Church, Roath Park. Finally, a huge diolch to my loving and endlessly patient family – to Lukas, Lena, Macsen Iago, and, of course, my incredible wife, Sandra. Ich liebe dich meine Familie.

*Who would have thought my shrivel'd heart*
*Could have recover'd greenness? It was gone*
*Quite underground…*
*And now in age I bud again,*
*After so many deaths I live and write*

George Herbert

# Prologue

*When you come to a new place, you tell your tale; the story of where you came from and how you got here, because that is the story of who you are.*

Kate Clanchy, poet

*Life can only be understood backwards; but it must be lived forwards.*

Søren Kierkegaard, philosopher

## The first step

'The beginning is the most important part of any work', wrote Plato in *The Republic*. The same could also be said of pilgrimage. The importance of that first, decisive step cannot be overstated – it requires courage, determination and unwavering commitment. While some may doubt the value of spiritual journeys, the pilgrim steps forward with excitement and hope, drawn by the adventure and mystery that await. As I stood in the grounds of the medieval Basingwerk Abbey in Flintshire, North Wales, and threw my rucksack over my shoulder, I took the first stride of a 140-mile journey that countless other pilgrims had walked over many centuries. In that moment, I felt connected not only to the path ahead but also to the footsteps of those who had travelled it before me, each carrying their own hopes, struggles and prayers.

In the weeks leading up to my journey, I could not help but share my planned odyssey with anyone who would listen. Each time someone praised my courage, their words served as a reminder that this was to be no ordinary walk. Yet nothing could have truly readied me for the sheer physical and emotional toll of the three relentless weeks of walking. And, as it turned out, the real challenge was not the miles travelled. Rather, it was the gruelling journey that awaited me in the months that followed. The first step of my pilgrimage may have been the most important, but it was far from the hardest part.

## Journeys of faith

In recent years, pilgrimage has experienced a remarkable resurgence, capturing the interest of people from all walks of life. This revival has been particularly evident in my own country of Wales, where significant investment has been made to restore and develop ancient pilgrim routes, drawing more walkers than at any time since the Reformation. Beyond the physical and mental rewards of these journeys, there is something deeply moving about following in the footsteps of saints who walked these paths centuries ago. The renewed fascination with pilgrimage has even made its way on to our screens. The BBC documentary series *Pilgrimage* has brought the experience to an even wider audience, as celebrities from diverse backgrounds lace up their boots, shoulder their backpacks and set out on famous routes. Along the way, they share their stories, wrestle with questions of faith and explore whether these age-old paths still hold meaning for believers and non-believers today.

Anthropologists suggest that spiritual journeys stretch back far beyond the well-worn paths we walk today. Some even argue that pilgrimage has evolutionary roots, echoing the ancient migrations of birds and animals. From humanity's earliest days, journeying was essential, whether for survival, as our hunter-gatherer ancestors roamed in search of food and warmth, or for faith, as seen in sacred texts like the Old and New Testaments. Pilgrimage reached its height of popularity in the West during the Middle Ages, when the church encouraged believers to travel in search of divine connection, forgiveness and atonement. In fact, even the modern package holiday owes its origins to religious travel, with 19th-century entrepreneur Thomas Cook building his global travel empire by organising trips for Christian pilgrims to the Holy Land.

Pilgrimage, though, has not always been welcomed and encouraged. From 16th-century Protestant reformers to 20th-century communist leaders, powerful figures have tried to suppress it. Still people found ways to journey, whether by visiting ancient shrines secretly and without fanfare or by taking secular pilgrimages to places like Lenin's tomb in Red Square or Mao Zedong's mausoleum in Tiananmen Square. No matter the obstacles, pilgrimage has endured. It seems to be woven into the fabric of who we are.

## The Pilgrim's Way

The Pilgrim's Way in North Wales was a path I had longed to tread for many years. As a teenager I had been obsessed with surfing. Growing up on the North Wales coast, my favourite surf spot was the breathtaking four-mile sandy bay called Porth Neigwl, located on the far western tip of North Wales, at the end of the Llŷn Peninsula. I would camp with a friend at the top of the cliff, waking early to clamber down to hit the huge waves that would pound the shore. The English name for the bay is Hell's Mouth, as it appears as an ominous orifice and has been, historically, a place of great danger to sailors during storms. After an exhilarating day's surfing, my friend and I would then drive up to the top of the not-so-imaginatively named Mynydd Mawr (Big Mountain) to watch the sun setting on the beautiful Ynys Enlli (Bardsey Island).

This isolated island became a magical and mystical place in my mind – my dad would talk about going there on pilgrimage in his youth and my ornithologist brother would encamp there to track bird migration. As I began to study history at university, I became fascinated with the island's ancient past. Neolithic people lived in stone huts on the island over 4,000 years ago, and it almost certainly already held spiritual significance by then.

Its importance as a Christian site began when early persecuted Christians were said to have hidden there to escape pagan oppressors. By the end of the sixth century, St Cadfan had established his monastery there. In the Middle Ages, Pope Callixtus II declared the island to be one of the most holy sites in Britain. It was considered so sacred that dying on the island was believed to guarantee sainthood and immediate entrance into heaven. There were even times when coffins were carried over in relays to the island, in the hope that being buried in its soil had the same effect as dying there.

It was during my surfing years when I first heard about the Pilgrim's Way. This is a medieval pilgrimage route running along the top of North Wales, from Basingwerk Abbey, the medieval monastery near Holywell, to Ynys Enlli, off the coast of Hell's Mouth. As a teenager, I felt certain that one day I would tread in the footsteps of those early pilgrims.

As it transpired, it was to be many years before I was able to undertake that journey. At first, work got in the way, as I was unable to secure three consecutive weeks of leave to complete the journey. Soon, though, it was neither time nor work but my injured body that prevented me from embarking on this endeavour. In my early 30s, I had suffered a serious back injury and underwent spinal surgery. A titanium bolt was inserted in the base of the spine to stabilise my back. Two years later, the excruciating pain was continuing to impede almost every part of my life, and I was hospitalised again in the Royal National Orthopaedic Hospital in London. There I undertook a four-week course of intensive physiotherapy, pain management and occupational therapy, which included being taught such basics as how, in a light of a back disability, to clean the bathroom, vacuum the house and wash dishes. While I was subsequently able to live a relatively normal life, my spinal trauma resulted in daily chronic pain and continuing disability, with standing still or sitting for any length of time causing considerable discomfort.

# Pilgrimage preparation

In building up fitness through hiking, Pilates and physiotherapy, I arrived at a place where my back seemed sufficiently strong to embark on the journey I had longed to undertake for decades. I also had the incredible opportunity to apply for a three-month sabbatical from work, a chance I could not pass up. My plan was ambitious, yet I was sure it would be deeply fulfilling. I was to spend the first three weeks walking the 140-mile Pilgrim's Way, immersing myself in its history and spiritual significance. Then, with two whole months ahead of me, I would embark on an exhilarating journey across the country, visiting ancient religious sites from Lindisfarne to the Orkneys. Having three months away from work felt like an extraordinary gift, and I could not wait for the adventure ahead. I was certain this time would be both inspiring and spiritually transformative.

As the Pilgrim's Way had recently been relaunched, it was an opportune time to take up its challenge. White waymarker disks had been erected intermittently along the trail, making use of existing public rights of way. The path traverses the dramatic, rolling hills of the Clwydian Range, the sweeping Conwy Valley with its majestic river, the breathtaking Eryri (Snowdonia) National Park in the shadow of the highest peak in England and Wales, Yr Wyddfa (Snowdon), and the spectacular sea views of the Wales Coast Path. The trail also takes in countless ancient stone churches, dedicated to prominent Celtic saints, which provide shelter and rest along the way. At these churches, and in some post offices and cafes, pilgrims can pause to stamp their 'Pilgrim Passport'. The stamps, designed by local primary school children, detail the ancient landmarks, legends and sites encountered on the trail.

And so it was that I committed myself to undertaking this arduous trek on foot. I prepared as best I could. Hailing from inclement North Wales, I knew the importance of good waterproof clothing. I also studied Ordnance Survey maps in great detail and trained my body with daily walks, leading to an increasing obsession with the step count on my Fitbit. No matter how carefully we plan, though, pilgrimage always holds an element of the unknown. We cannot predict the people we will meet, the lessons we will learn or the twists the journey will take. Most of all, until we take that first step, the significant challenges ahead remain hidden, waiting to unfold.

## The six pilgrimage experiences

In hindsight, it was apt that the pilgrimage began in the twelfth-century Besingwerk Abbey. On the one hand, its impressive frame is a testament to the beautiful rich tapestry of faith held by our ancestors. On the other hand, the abbey is now an empty shell, which intimates only something small of its glorious past. As such, its crumbling walls are a stark reminder of the inhumanity, pain and suffering of the past, not least in the dissolution of the monasteries during the 16th-century Reformation. Such ruins, as travel writer Nick Mayhew-Smith puts it, 'bear witness to just as much anger and destruction as they do to love and devotion; they are places with a history of death, of mourning, of desecration'. My pilgrimage was to mirror the history of Basingwerk Abbey. The walk was not to be about joy and wonder alone. Rather, it was to take me to dark, distressing and depressing places. Furthermore, in the months after hiking the Pilgrim's Way, I would be forced to tread a second journey in which I would face a very different 'Hell's Mouth'.

As my North Wales pilgrimage came to an end, I crossed to Ynys Enlli on a calm and crystalline sea. I had no way of knowing the storms that would await me upon my return home. Very soon I was forced to confront a serious relapse of my spinal injury, a struggle made heavier by the looming shadow of depression and anxiety that so often accompanies the loss of health. The peace of Enlli felt distant as I was pulled into the depths of pain, uncertainty and helplessness.

I have come to see that second journey of injury and recovery also as a pilgrimage. Spiritual journeys, after all, share certain core elements. While the depth of pilgrimage cannot be fully contained, there are six distinct experiences that could be said to define such sacred travels:

suffering, wonder, signs, company, dependence and hope. This book is, therefore, not a chronological memoir, unfolding as a narrative, full of twists and revelations. In fact, you will know the ending from the very beginning. Instead, it takes a reflective approach, exploring each of these six pilgrimage experiences in turn. By doing so, it will invite us to attune our eyes and ears to God's presence in our own journeys. The chapters are shaped by my two very different pilgrimages: the first, the physical journey across North Wales, and the second, a journey of healing undertaken from the confines of my sofa. Each chapter will alternate between these two contexts as they are divided to reflect on each journey separately, offering insights from both.

We begin the first chapter with adversity and *suffering*, which can so often permeate pilgrimage. If the book were to end there, though, it would leave us with a bleak picture of life's journeys. Thankfully, suffering is only part of the story. Pilgrimage offers other experiences that are vivid, life-transforming and filled with grace.

In the second chapter, we will explore the sense of *wonder* found in our journeys and consider how the beauty of the natural world and sacred places stirs something deep within us.

The third chapter focuses on '*signs*', those unexpected moments when God's presence breaks through, lifting us and leaving us awestruck.

The fourth chapter highlights the significance of *company*, celebrating the often-unlikely mix of friends and strangers who journey with us. These people remind us of the central role of love and support in our lives.

Building on this, the fifth chapter examines our *dependence* on others and the importance of gratitude as we navigate our lives.

Finally, in the sixth chapter, we arrive at *hope*, which lies at the foundation of all our journeys. Hope weaves through our joys and struggles, infusing even the most ordinary moments with meaning and purpose. Hope is the thread that holds our journeys together.

## Embracing our own pilgrimages

In exploring these six profound experiences that shaped my two journeys, this book also invites you to see your own paths as sacred and transformative pilgrimages. At times, you may be taken over literal mountains and through literal valleys, as you embrace physical pilgrimages. More often, though, the landscapes you navigate will be the unseen terrain of life's journeys.

So, as you read, consider the journey you are on right now. Perhaps it is a journey through *illness* or *recovery*, where uncertainty and struggle weigh heavy. Or the path of *vocation*, as you seek to discern God's calling. Or the daily rhythm of *work*, where you strive to find meaning in your labour. Or the journey of *education*, as you stretch your mind and grow through study. Or the passage of *faith*, as you wrestle with questions and deepen your beliefs. Or the journey of *family life*, as you pour yourself into the people you love. Or perhaps you are simply using this book to help you journey through *Lent* or *Advent*. Or maybe you relate to more than one!

All of your journeys can be seen as pilgrimages in themselves, shaping and transforming you, and, as you read, you will recognise the six experiences explored in this book shining through them. In each chapter of the book, following the exploration of my two journeys, a third section will help you to pause and consider your journeys, finishing with some questions to guide your personal reflection. You will be encouraged to encounter the struggle of suffering, the wonder of God's presence, signs that guide you, strength from those who walk beside you and humble reminders of your dependence on others. And through it all, you can open yourselves to the hope that redeems each step you take. By recognising these experiences in our own journeys, we not only come to understand ourselves more deeply, but we also begin to see where the light of God's grace is breaking through to illuminate our paths. In those moments, transformation happens, and we are drawn ever closer to becoming all that God intends us to be.

While the third section of each chapter, which concludes with questions for reflection, invites you to explore your own journey more personally, the book also includes a concise study guide at the end. This can be used for deeper individual exploration or as a resource for small group discussion, whether during Lent, Advent or any other season. The guide offers questions designed to help you think more deeply about the paths you are walking and to encourage meaningful conversation when meeting with others. It also includes suggested prayers to help bring your time to a thoughtful close. Whether you are reflecting alone or with others, it is hoped that these resources open your heart to the gentle unfolding of God's presence in your journeys.

## Journeys of transformation

Kierkegaard compared Abraham's arduous journey up and down Mount Moriah (Genesis 22:1–19) to a pilgrimage. The patriarch's travels, which included that shocking divine instruction to sacrifice his beloved son Isaac, involved much anxiety, struggle and suffering. But he eventually, in Kierkegaard's words, 'headed home joyously, cheerfully, with trust in God'. It was a profoundly transformative event that left an indelible mark on him. He returned to Beersheba with a transformed perspective on relationships, not least his relationship with the transcendent. He had, after all, witnessed God's provision firsthand, and this reaffirmed his trust and faith in God as Father.

Similarly, I found myself profoundly transfigured through both my North Wales pilgrimage and my journey of injury and recovery. My ordinary, everyday life was deeply affected by the people I encountered, the experiences I underwent and the places I visited, both literally and metaphorically. My journeys involved struggle and suffering, but, like Abraham's ascent and descent of Moriah, they also paradoxically reinforced my trust in God's care, love and provision.

As such, on so many levels, philosopher Charles Foster's description of pilgrimages as 'the ultimate otherness' rings true. Both of my journeys felt like surreal desert experiences, marked by exhilarating highs and crushing lows. Both pushed me beyond the familiar, forcing me to wrestle with life's deepest questions. They challenged me to confront, and even question, my intimate relationship with God. Yet, in both, he met me in my wilderness, bringing redemption, renewal and the promise of resurrection. My whole being was awakened as his love reached me in such unexpected ways. And, slowly but surely, the barrenness of Lent and the agony of Holy Week gave way to the triumphant, life-affirming hope of Easter Sunday.

## TIME TO REFLECT

- Think back to any physical pilgrimages you've taken – where did you go and why?

- What other kinds of journeys are you on in your life right now?

- As you read this book, take time to reflect on both the physical pilgrimages you have made and the personal or spiritual journeys you are currently navigating.

# 1

# Suffering

*Suffering is having what you don't want or wanting what you don't have.*

Elisabeth Elliot, missionary and author

*They can only come to morning through the shadows.*

J.R.R. Tolkien, author

## JOURNEY ONE: PILGRIM'S WAY

### There may be troubles ahead

All journeys come with their share of trials and challenges. For pilgrims, though, struggle is not viewed as a burden, but as an essential part of the adventure, embraced as a test of both strength and spirit. Yet, the hurdles braved by most contemporary pilgrims seem rather insignificant when we peer back through the centuries. Historically, pilgrims regularly faced kidnapping, robbery and physical violence. Knowing that these extreme hardships of pilgrimage are relics of a distant past, it is easy to underestimate just how demanding a pilgrimage can still be in the 21st century. I had envisaged something romantic about the trials and tribulations that I was to face. I imagined myself as a struggling lone traveller gazing at breathtaking scenery from the summit of a mountain. But the reality was far less poetic and far more challenging in ways I had not anticipated. Every step tested my resolve. Though they were far from the life-threatening dangers faced by pilgrims in centuries past, the hardships I encountered were still a formidable test of both body and spirit.

The biggest challenge of my pilgrimage began before I even stepped out the front door of my house. Hours of sitting at my desk, battling my overflowing email inbox, took their toll on one of my knees. At first it simply felt somewhat irritated and sore, but, by the first morning of the pilgrimage, it was inflamed and throbbing with pain. I found myself at a metaphorical crossroads, asking whether to push forward with the walk or to abandon it and turn back home to Cardiff. I called a physiotherapist friend to ask his advice. He quickly diagnosed patellar tendinitis. While this is undoubtedly a painful condition, he reassured me that continuing the trek would not cause lasting damage. The choice was mine.

It felt unthinkable, though, to turn back now. I had taken a sabbatical to embark on this walk, and I was set to raise a significant amount for charity. I therefore refused to let this setback derail everything before I had even begun. My mother suggested a walking stick to help me navigate the countless stiles along the route. What started as a practical aid soon became a constant and necessary companion. Over time, it took on a deeper, spiritual significance. Walking sticks have long symbolised faith and hope in the Christian tradition. As I leaned on mine for support, it became more than just a tool – it was a reminder of perseverance and trust in something greater. As the pain intensified, I found myself clinging to that conviction just as tightly as I gripped the handle.

## Crossing generations

As I followed the ancient route, the increasing pain in my knee became more than just a personal struggle. Instead, it connected me to the countless pilgrims who had walked this same path before me, each carrying their own burdens. Suffering, after all, is timeless. It weaves the past and present together, a shared human experience across generations. I was reminded of A.E. Housman's 'On Wenlock Edge', where the poet stands gazing over the Shropshire hills, weighed down by his troubles. He takes comfort in the thought that nearly 2,000 years earlier, a Roman soldier may have stood on that very same spot, wrestling with similar fears and emotions. Pain, whether physical or emotional, is never endured alone, but it echoes through history:

> *There, like the wind through woods in riot,*
> *Through him the gale of life blew high;*
> *The tree of man was never quiet:*
> *Then 'twas the Roman, now 'tis I.*

That poem lingered in my mind as I paused at sacred sites along the Pilgrim's Way, where countless seekers before me had come in search of healing. Some were weathered crosses in silent churchyards, while others were ancient holy wells, their waters steeped in centuries of faith and longing.

For our ancestors, natural springs held particular significance. Unlike statues or megaliths, wells could not be destroyed and, tapping into underground sources, they provided clean, safe water. They would have been a precious gift at a time when rivers and streams were often contaminated with human and animal waste, carrying deadly diseases. Over time, these enduring wells came to be seen as vessels of divine power. Stories of miraculous healings at such springs began to spread. Their origins stretched back to pre-Christian times, but it was during the era of the early Celtic saints that these wondrous tales truly flourished, growing ever more frequent. It is no coincidence that the words 'healthy', 'whole' and 'holy' all share the same root in the English language, derived from *halig*, the Saxon word for holy. These wells were more than just sources of water; they were believed to hold a divine power to restore both body and soul. They were holy, healing wells.

# Holy wells and healing crosses

Shortly after setting out from Basingwerk Abbey, I arrived at the first, and most famous, well along the trail. St Winefride's Well in Holywell, often called 'the Lourdes of Wales', is the only shrine in the British Isles with an unbroken history stretching back to the eighth century. Standing at its sacred waters, I took a moment to pray, asking for healing for the pain in my knee. For centuries, pilgrims had come here seeking miracles. At the entrance stood a striking testament to its history – a stack of crutches from every era, left behind by pilgrims who had walked away restored. Pilgrims have long followed two sacred rituals here, either immersing themselves three times in the water, echoing an ancient Celtic tradition, or wading around the well's edge while reciting the rosary. I chose a simpler path. Rather than plunging in, I simply sat at the water's edge, gently splashing my aching knee and offering a silent prayer for strength and healing.

Such prayer became a regular routine at holy wells and healing crosses I passed along the way, each in places with beautiful names in equally beautiful countryside, including at Tremeirchion, Llangelynnin and Clynnog Fawr. At the wells, the routine became a ceremony in itself – pulling up my trouser leg, dowsing my knee with water, and silently petitioning God for strength and relief. Shrines always carry the risk of shifting focus away from God, sometimes even fostering superstition, commercialism or exploitation. Yet in the places I visited, these dangers felt distant. Instead, the wells and crosses functioned as icons, leading me to contemplate the divine and experience a palpable presence of the Spirit.

Though I felt a deep spiritual connection at these sacred places, the pain in my knee refused to fade. On the steep ascents and descents, the rugged terrain showed no mercy. At times, I found myself limping through the miles, each step a test of endurance. While prayer at holy sites may not have brought about a miraculous cure, it certainly gave me the strength and focus to press on. As such, I was walking in the footsteps of countless suffering pilgrims who had travelled this same path before me. Many would still be carrying a physical or emotional limp at the end of their journey, some still locked in the struggle of chronic pain or disability. And yet, for so many, the pilgrimage will have blessed them with something deeper – a healing of the soul that went beyond the hope of a bodily cure.

## A word on the stone

Yet physical pain was just one obstacle on this journey. Countless other challenges tested my resolve, each one slowing my progress and chipping away at my energy and patience – inclement weather, thick mud, electric fences, barking dogs, threatening cows, dense fog, fallen trees, collapsed pathways and waymarker signs that were in disrepair, hidden or vandalised. When I arrived at Aberdaron, the final stop before sailing to Ynys Enlli, I felt deserving of the free meal I had been told that pilgrims could claim at the not-so-imaginatively named restaurant: Y Gegin Fawr (The Big Kitchen). I was, though, informed that I was 400 years too late to take advantage of this tradition. Contemporary business models do not, apparently, factor in free meals as rewards for lengthy spiritual journeys! I therefore had to pay for my omelette and chips.

After satiating my hunger at this 14th-century establishment, I wandered to a much newer building, the Porth y Swnt visitor centre. Here, pilgrims are invited to inscribe their thoughts onto stones, adding them to a growing 'sea of words'. These chalk-marked stones capture what the journey to the tip of the Llŷn Peninsula means to travellers.

I spent time meditating on the words written on the many stones in this ambitious bilingual brainstorming session. The words were, by and large, positive and uplifting – peace, happiness, tranquillity, love, hope, stillness, nature, happiness, inspiring and so on. By now, I was painfully aware that pilgrimage had a more difficult and challenging side and so I added my own word – 'suffering'. After all, my journey along the Pilgrim's Way had been marked by relentless challenges, slow and frustrating progress, and more than a few moments when I was tempted to give up. But these difficulties would pale into comparison with the pain and struggle of the very different pilgrimage I would tread in the months after joyously stepping off the ferry onto Enlli's holy ground.

# JOURNEY TWO: THROUGH INJURY AND DARKNESS

## A second pilgrimage begins

The tendinitis in my knee had been excruciating throughout the walk, forcing me to limp for most of the long trek. Yet, despite this, my long-standing spinal condition had remained stable. After the triumph of setting foot on Enlli's sacred ground on the final day of the pilgrimage, I went to bed on a high, exhausted but elated. But the moment I woke the next morning, I knew something was wrong. The twinge I could feel in my back was different from the chronic pain I had learned to live with. Instead, it was a sensation I recognised instantly, and it catapulted me back twelve years to the darkest days of the injury that had led to major back surgery. The ache in my lower back was soon accompanied by increasing numbness and burning down my left leg. Over the next few days, the discomfort worsened, as my body started signalling that something was seriously wrong. Within a fortnight, the pain had escalated to an unbearable level, confirming what I had feared: this was a relapse of the injury I had convinced myself was behind me. My second pilgrimage had begun.

Over the next few months, MRI scans revealed the harsh reality that I was struggling with three degenerated discs, each in varying stages of prolapse. As I processed the news, I found myself reflecting on the exhilaration and exertion of my 140-mile journey. Humans are born to walk. When life overwhelms us, we instinctively set one foot in front of the other. 'Every day I walk myself into a state of well-being and walk away from every illness', wrote Kierkegaard. Yet, within weeks of returning from my trek, I could barely make it to the end of the road. Sitting and standing became agonising battles, and walking, once my refuge, was painfully limited. My world shrank to the confines of my red sofa, where I spent most of my days lying down, rising only to press an ice pack against my spine or for brief, painful walks in the garden.

As a vicar of a large church, I was keenly aware that my own struggles seemed insignificant compared to the immense hardships others endure. Over the years, I have stood beside people in the depths of unimaginable suffering, feeling powerless as I comforted those shattered by heartbreaking grief and devastating diagnoses. Yet I also knew that suffering is deeply personal. As a former university chaplain, I have watched students spiral into despair over heartbreak, exam failures or the fear of an uncertain future, struggles that others might dismiss as trivial. To those students, though, their pain was as real and consuming as any other. Psychologist Viktor Frankl, who endured the horrors of the Nazi death camps, warned against measuring or comparing suffering. Instead, he insisted that *all* pain be taken seriously. Suffering, he explained, is like gas released into an empty chamber – it expands to fill the space entirely. In other words, the 'size' of suffering is relative. No matter how 'big' or 'small' suffering appears from the outside, it has the power to consume us completely.

## Mind games

Regardless of the physical pain we endure, the impact of adversity always extends far beyond physical pain. Frankl refers to 'Sunday neurosis', a phrase alluding to the emptiness that surfaces inside us when the busyness of our working week subsides. This is when melancholy can seep into our lives. With my injury, my former busy life was brought to a sharp halt. I thought back to the time I was preparing for my North Wales pilgrimage. Life had seemed so colourful, joyful and vibrant. Yet now, as I lost all perspective, life seemed uncompromisingly bleak. As I lay at home in pain, a storm of irrational and self-destructive emotions took hold. I could not shake the thought that I had brought this suffering upon myself by choosing to embark on such a physically demanding pilgrimage. I knew that dwelling on regret only made things worse, not just for me but for those around me, not least my wife and children, who became collateral damage to my inner turmoil. But there was a disconnect between my desire to stop such depressive thought patterns and my ability to do so.

The searing pain in my back and legs was relentless, but the tricks my mind played made everything infinitely worse. At the start of *The Divine Comedy*, Dante describes reaching the midpoint of his life's journey, only to find himself lost in a dark and menacing wood, 'scarcely less bitter than death'. I could not help but recall my own moments of being lost in the forests of North Wales during my pilgrimage, battered by driving rain and howling wind, desperately searching for the right path.

But now I faced an even greater challenge – a descent into the tangled, merciless woods of depression and anxiety. As I catastrophised about my future, the fear of what *might* happen loomed far larger than what *was* happening. While recovering from his own back surgery, actor Michael J. Fox compared his experience of dwelling in the depths of fear to being on safari. The worse part of safari, he wrote, is 'worrying about the leopards we can't see'. He recollects feeling safe in his 4x4 jeep, despite the genuine threat of the leopards walking past. However, when the vehicle broke down and he had to wait to be rescued, the leopards hidden in the surrounding shrubbery suddenly felt like a real threat: 'It's that gut feeling that something is wrong, very wrong. Something is out there waiting to pounce. No warning, no negotiation, no accommodation.' Things that are imagined can sometimes have far more of a hold on us than the obvious and visible threats.

And so, each night, as I lay awake for hours, I was trapped in an endless cycle of fearful and pessimistic thoughts that refused to be silenced. The weight of it all felt unbearable and it began to chip away at my self-worth. Too often our society regards ability and productivity as the basis of personal worth. The young, healthy and athletic are glorified on television, in magazines and on our social media feeds. When our health fails, though, it can become a savage reminder that our society defines us on what we do and achieve. As I lay in pain on my sofa, not 'doing' anything, I found myself like Dorothy in *The Wizard of Oz*, longing to return to the comfort of the life I used to have. Yet unlike Dorothy, whose longing was to return home, I was stuck at home, leaving only for very short, pain-filled walks. Albert Ellis, the founder of rational emotive behaviour therapy, argues that, while adversity is a part of life, 'suffering' begins when we convince ourselves that our struggles define our worth. As the months passed by, I started to believe that my pain was defining my very being. As I trod my second pilgrimage, I was learning that pain is not simply something to be endured; it has the relentless power to unravel a person, thought by thought.

## The random cruelty of pain

The rollercoaster of dark emotions that swirled around in my head punctured my long-held belief that life made sense and that the world was orderly and stable. Suffering, after all, often comes to us out of the blue, unexpectedly tearing our lives apart. After conquering the deadly heights of the world's 14 highest peaks, explorer Reinhold Messner was seriously injured, not on an unforgiving mountainside, but at home, after scaling a wall to open a window because he had forgotten his keys. Few of us can foresee the moment that illness, injury, loss or grief will invade our lives. When it happens, it can feel as though our whole world is crumbling. Despite this, all around us life seems to be marching on – steady, indifferent and seemingly untouched by our personal chaos. As James Bryan Smith wrote, describing the heart-breaking and life-changing day his young daughter died:

> I remembered looking out from the third-floor window of the hospital room. The traffic below flowed on as if nothing had happened. The cars moved and stopped, and pulled into fast-food

restaurants or parking lots. People were crossing the street, talking and laughing. Don't they know what just happened?

Apart from the grief of my grandparents passing and the trauma of witnessing the impact of my mother's heartbreaking miscarriages, I was sheltered from suffering as a child. When I was 15 years old, though, its ruthless nature hit home. Our babysitter Nicholas, the son of my mother's closest friend, had brought so much light into my childhood. Only five years older than me, he was a person of mischief and fun whom I simply adored. Not long after he had left for university in the late 1980s, my mother sat on my bed one evening, her eyes filled with tears. In a trembling voice, she told me that Nicholas was in intensive care, struck down by the ruthless new disease that government adverts, with their grave voices and ominous gravestones, had been warning us about. Nicholas rallied and lived for a number of years with AIDS, and I was blessed to share some more joyful times with him. It was poignant that my North Wales pilgrimage took me past where Nicholas' ashes had been scattered, on the mountain behind Penmaenmawr. Looking back at my 15-year-old self as my mum broke the news of Nicholas' illness, this was the first time that I had to face the indiscriminate cruelty of suffering. Even at that young age, the theological consequences of the situation did not escape me – how does the heartbreaking pain and suffering I saw Nicholas and his family go through relate to a God of love and compassion?

Each of us will have our own moments in life when we face struggle and adversity – grief, injury, illness, the break-up of a relationship, depression, anxiety, unemployment or some other hardship. At other times, we stand alongside friends and family in their dark and despairing moments. Those of us involved in health care, social work or pastoral care will have seen suffering dehumanise and devastate individuals and families. Like other pastoral carers, I carry with me the agony and tears I have witnessed over the past decades: journeying alongside people in the final months of cancer, leukaemia and brain tumours; sitting with parents who had tragically lost children and children who had tragically lost parents; and praying with those affected by the suicide of a loved one or the unforgiving decline of a life partner with dementia. And yet, despite what I have witnessed or experienced, and despite many years of studying theodicy and the theology of pain, suffering feels as alien and confusing to me as it did when, at the age of 15, my mother sat on my bed to break the traumatic news of Nicholas' condition.

## The mystery of suffering

Many centuries of philosophical musing from all religious and secular traditions have shown suffering is not an intellectual challenge that becomes more comprehensible as we contemplate it. It cannot be viewed as a conundrum to be solved. But regarding suffering as a foe to be defeated can be equally misguided. As a society, we are inclined to do this, albeit perhaps unconsciously.

We often use, for example, conqueror imagery in relation to facing our difficulties. In my pastoral work, I have regularly heard people use phrases such as 'they battled hard', 'they fought a brave fight' or 'they lost their battle' to describe facing a disease or condition. While this can seem comforting for those involved, a growing number of psychologists are questioning the appropriateness of using such metaphors. In any battle or fight there are winners and losers and, in light of how suffering dehumanises and ravages, speaking in such terms can be alienating and hurtful to those who are facing adversity. As early as the 1970s, Susan Sontag, the prominent American critic, noted that wrapping suffering in metaphors has no bearing on the reality of pain. Rather, it can have the effect of discouraging, silencing and shaming those who are facing hardships. More recently, Sunita Puri, the director of the Hospice and Palliative Medicine Fellowship at the University of Massachusetts, called for the battle metaphor to be jettisoned in medicine as it can lead to the misplacing of blame for those living with terminal or chronic illness.

The French philosopher Gabriel Marcel suggests that, rather than either a problem or a foe, suffering must simply be viewed as a *mystère* ('mystery'). After all, suffering challenges our understanding and resists a simple explanation. As it is something that all humans participate in personally, it is impossible for us to step outside of it to analyse it objectively. It must, therefore, simply be embraced as a mystery, allowing it to deepen our relationships, our understanding of ourselves and our connection with God. Marcel notes that the one thing that gives suffering a redemptive power – love – is also a mystery. Both suffering and love can be experienced, but neither can be explained. It is love, shown in a practical way by those around us, that brings hope to our times of suffering and assures us of the presence of something greater than ourselves in our struggles.

On my second pilgrimage, I found comfort in Marcel's explanation of the dual mystery of the human condition. I was, though, still left grappling with what remains of us when suffering strips away those things that define us. This struggle lies at the heart of our existence and echoes throughout scripture, not least in the book of Job. I had my loving family and friends standing alongside me at this time, but so much else of what defined 'me' seemed lost. In looking to the future, it felt as if I was facing an unknown abyss.

# ON OUR JOURNEYS

## Dark nights of the soul

At some point in our lives, all of us will face events that lead to such existential turmoil. During my journey of recovery, I would undertake hydrotherapy sessions at the hospital. With each of us patients having been through various injuries, many quite serious, I was struck by the plethora of scars in the pool each week – on backs, shoulders, arms, knees and ankles. Yet, if we could peer into the souls of those around us, how many more deep-seated scars would we notice?

Kierkegaard noted that, during the times that leave us with physical and emotional scars, 'whoever has learned to be anxious in the right way has learned the ultimate'. He related his journey through the pilgrimage of pain to the Christian doctrine of original sin. The biblical story of Adam and Eve, he writes, is a dramatising of a fall that happens again and again during our lives. When we face suffering, we 'fall' through the 'sin' of relying on worldly relief, rather than on spiritual sustenance. Kierkegaard suggests that sin is not just a moral failing. Rather, it is a kind of spiritual disorientation, a turning away from God's grace in our moments of struggle. But as I slowly recovered, leaning on God felt like an uphill battle. Prayer became hollow, while meditation only stirred more unrest.

My feeling of separation from God was very much akin to what St John of the Cross described as the 'dark night of the soul'. Pain grinds us down and affects us spiritually, as well as physically and emotionally. Joy has always been integral to my faith. Christians are people of the 'good news' or 'gospel' (Greek: *euangelion*) and my own Welsh Christian heritage includes the wonderful concept of *hwyl*, a joyous and intense religious fervour. Yet, my pain and anxiety were taking me to a very different place, edging me towards negativity, cynicism and pessimism. As a sufferer of chronic pain, I had long been concerned that my natural optimism and joy would eventually begin to be drained away.

During my time at university, I explored how the failing health of 16th-century reformer Martin Luther may have played a role, however indirectly, in shaping the horrific anti-Semitic policies of the Third Reich. Nazi propagandists later cited Luther's hostile writings on Judaism in their pamphlets. Some historians believe his declining health was a key factor that led him to a drastic shift from his earlier, more tolerant stance towards the Jewish faith. As his pain worsened, so too did the tone of his theology, growing harsher, less tolerant and increasingly devoid of compassion towards other faiths.

Resisting hopelessness and bitterness during my journey of recovery was a constant challenge. And when we suffer, it is difficult, if not impossible, to hide the impact of these struggles from those around us. Most of us got used to wearing masks during the Covid pandemic. The reality is, though, that we wear metaphorical masks all the time. 'The mask is the way you manage what other people think of you,' writes James Bryan Smith; 'you let them see what you think they want to see, but they never get to see the real you.'

In our daily lives, we smoothly transition between different masks, adapting to the people around us and the roles we play. But suffering has a way of tearing those masks away, leaving us raw and exposed, revealing the 'real me'. With the relapse of my back injury, I could no longer present myself as strong, successful or in control. I remember a young ordinand and an older parishioner coming to visit. Normally, I was the one offering them support and counsel. But here I was, lying on my sofa, wracked with pain and unable to hold back tears. Stripped of pretence, I was no longer the strong, dependable pastor. I was the one in need, laid bare and utterly vulnerable.

## Where is God when we suffer?

It is little wonder that, for some, the presence of suffering makes it difficult to hold on to a loving God. In an interview on Irish television in 2015, the actor Stephen Fry famously described the divine as a 'capricious, mean-minded, stupid God who creates a world which is so full of injustice and pain'. Only a few weeks earlier, *The Theory of Everything* had opened in cinemas to widespread acclaim. Although an uplifting film which is full of hope and love, it is hard for viewers to escape feeling helpless and angry at the unjust pain and suffering on the screen. Not only does motor neurone disease ravage Professor Stephen Hawking's body, but we also witness the mental anguish of his family and friends, as they face the consequences of an unforgiving terminal disease. There is certainly no 'theory of everything' for Christians to explain the presence of pain in the world. In the face of the devastating impact suffering has on us, it would be appropriate for the Christian to scream to heaven in outrage and indignation. This is affirmed in scripture, especially in the psalms, which encourage us to lay bare all human experiences and emotions before our Father God, not least our pain, despair, questioning and cries for help. 'The best prayers,' wrote John Bunyan, 'have often more groans than words.'

When confronted with the question of suffering, then, not only is intellectual satisfaction out of our reach, but challenging the divine becomes understandable and necessary. Both the biblical witness and Christian tradition teach that we can find and feel God's presence in the midst of this protest. In recognising the divine presence here, though, we are again taken back to a deep and unfathomable mystery. After all, in the book of Job, possibly the oldest book in the Bible, God gives no answer to the problem of pain. Instead, he responds to Job's cries about the mystery of suffering with divine mystery, highlighting all the beauty and wonder he has created.

Even the biblical arc is a wonderful pattern of this divine, redemptive mystery – creation, incarnation, crucifixion, resurrection and final glorious consummation. At the crux of this mystery stands the cross (Latin: *crux*). The glorious symbol of the Christian faith is a powerful symbol of pain and suffering. But it is also the symbol of that other great mystery – love. *In* the cross, we are reassured that love and suffering are intimately related. *On* the cross, we are taught something that human parents also instinctively know – that sacrifice, suffering and love are all intertwined.

When I was suffering back pain, I found myself drawing parallels with Christ's path to the cross, the *Via dolarosa*. There is something profoundly transformative in recognising Jesus' suffering within our own trials. It is precisely because God knows what it is like to suffer that he stands alongside us in our physical and emotional distress. In our darkest moments, we encounter a God who not only understands our pain but also shares in it. And so the question of whether there is divine purpose *in* suffering may well be a fruitless one to ask; for the Christian, the question of whether there is divine redemption *of* suffering carries far greater significance.

## Crucified and resurrected

An emphasis on the cross alone, though, will lead to an imbalanced faith. The Easter triduum is not simply about the pain of Good Friday and the darkness of Holy Saturday. Theologian Miroslav Volf reminds us that the real mystery of God is that he is both the crucified one *and* the resurrected one. We cannot have one without the other. As the crucified one, his presence is in the midst of our suffering, listening to our anguished cries and wiping our tears. As the resurrected one, he is present in every compassionate act and each moment of self-sacrifice. In a nutshell, concludes Volf, 'God suffers and God helps'. This profound truth can bring freedom and liberation when our hearts ache for a sign of God's presence in the midst of relentless pain or deep despair. It reminds us that suffering is never the end of the story and that redemption and renewal are always at work in our lives.

While many see the world's tragedies as proof against a loving God, my journey was taking me in a different direction. Pain and suffering only truly make sense in the light of love and compassion. Ours is a God who does not remain distant from our anguish but enters into it, standing beside us when we cry out in despair or protest. He may not offer easy answers, but through his presence, he does offer his hope and meaning, even in the most hopeless and meaningless moments.

As such, as I lay in physical and emotional pain, I began to recognise the absolute necessity of moving through the question of 'Why me?' to arrive at the more important question of 'Where is he?' It became clear that I needed to shift my perspective on this second pilgrimage. In particular, I needed to open my eyes to glimpse the glimmers of God's light shining through the other profound experiences that are related to spiritual journeys – wonder, signs, company, dependence and hope.

Only a week before leaving for my North Wales walk, I had spoken to an elderly parishioner who was terminally ill. 'I'm not scared of death,' he told me. 'In fact, I'm actually excited about the next stage of my adventure.' His positivity, especially in light of such a bleak diagnosis, stayed with me. As I wiled away my days on my red sofa, the pull of fear, regret and despair was strong. At times, it was almost suffocating. But my faith began to reassure me that Jesus' crucifixion and resurrection offered a deeper truth. His is a light that refuses to be swallowed by darkness and a hope that defies even the most hopeless of circumstances.

Towards the end of *The Theory of Everything*, as Stephen Hawking and his wife grapple with the pain of separation, he looks at her, both of them in tears, and quietly says four simple words – 'Everything will be okay.' When we face suffering, those words can feel impossible to hold on to. Yet, their quiet mystery lies at the heart of the Christian response to pain. From Jesus himself through countless Christian thinkers down the ages, from Julian of Norwich to Dietrich Bonhoeffer, this hope has echoed through the centuries, not as a denial of suffering, but as a promise that, even in our darkest moments, God's love is at work.

## TIME TO REFLECT

- Take a moment to reflect on times of pain or suffering you've experienced – what physical or emotional scars do you carry with you on life's journey?

- As you think about the path you are on right now, where do you see God meeting you in your struggles?

- How might God's love be at work, even in the hardest moments?

# 2

# Wonder

---

*We are surrounded by a world that talks, but we don't listen. We are part of a community engaged in a vast conversation, but we deny our role in it.*

Belden Lane, theologian

*Above all, watch with glittering eyes the whole world around you because the greatest secrets are always hidden in the most unlikely places.*

Roald Dahl, children's author

## JOURNEY ONE: PILGRIM'S WAY

### Pilgrimage and nature

Writing of his walk from John O'Groats to Land's End, philosopher Gary Hayden explores how attitudes to nature of those walking in the countryside can differ. Someone merely out for a stroll, he writes, has nothing in common with the fauna and flora that they pass. A tree, for example, will be simply a wild thing considered by a tame person – both exist separately. However, for those trekking for long periods, whether on a pilgrimage or a long hike, a special connection with nature is forged. The pilgrim and the tree they pass have been scorched by the same sun, swept by the same wind and soaked by the same rain. They have a kindred existence. 'On a day walk, you're a tourist, an observer, of nature,' he concludes, 'but, on a long-distance walk, you become part of nature.'

The difficulties faced on a pilgrimage would be bleak and hopeless if they stood alone. Thankfully, journeys also offer moments that transcend adversity and ground us in the beauty and blessing of God's creation. In this sense, pilgrimages can be epiphanic, revealing God's presence and wonder, and incarnational, as our senses are open to experiencing the universal Christ all around us. As the Eastern Orthodox classic *The Way of a Pilgrim* puts it:

> Not only was I experiencing deep interior joy, but I sensed a oneness with all of God's creation; people, animals, trees, and plants all seemed to have the name of Jesus Christ imprinted upon them.

During my North Wales pilgrimage, I felt increasingly immersed in my surroundings and became aware of the natural world in an intimate way, from the macro scale of the breathtaking landscapes to the micro scale of the plants and flowers at my feet. The 19th-century poet John Clare wrote about dropping down to nature, suggesting that we sit or lie down to experience the natural world from its own viewpoint. I took this to heart and would regularly stop and lie down, whether in a forest, on a beach or in a field, drinking in the heady atmosphere of the natural world. By doing so, I embraced the holy here-and-now. My eyes were opened to a world that was not mechanical, inanimate and expendable, but was brimming with sacred life.

## Communicating with the natural world

Some pilgrims speak of feeling so deeply connected to nature that they begin to converse with the wildlife around them. On my own journey, I found myself greeting animals and birds, sometimes in English or Welsh, but often by mimicking their own sounds, whether bleating to the sheep or cooing to the wood pigeons. At times, it felt as though they were responding. Even in their silence, though, their very existence seemed to be speaking to me. Meister Eckhart wrote that all living and created things are 'words of God', reflecting his wisdom, love and creativity. As such, I was witness to a divine conversation written in the language of nature.

Before my pilgrimage, I would have been taken aback by a pilgrim admitting that they, like a modern-day Dr Dolittle, talked to creatures on their journey. Infants often anthropomorphise the natural world, giving animals and birds character, personality and even personhood. Our childhood stories, from Narnia to the Gruffalo, are filled with talking creatures. I began to recapture something of this childlike inclination in my pilgrimage communication with wildlife and, slowly but surely, I felt as if I was becoming an intimate part of my surroundings.

In past centuries, such a deep bond with nature was simply a way of life. But in modern times, we often view the natural world through a more detached lens. Pilgrimages offer a chance to reclaim something older and more instinctive – a harmonious connection with nature that feels both refreshing and authentic. In the Bible, God's kingdom is sometimes described as being where animals live in harmony, even ones that are usually hostile to one another (see Isaiah 11:6; 65:25). I certainly felt as if something of God's kingdom was present as I stared into the eyes of seals as they emerged from the waters below me, talked to squirrels who begged for crumbs as I stopped for lunch, gazed at gliding buzzards and swooping kestrels, and marvelled at dolphins leaping in the distant, crystal blue sea.

The connection with nature on pilgrimage goes beyond our connection with living creatures. The primatologist Jane Goodall reflected on her time in the wild jungle of Tanzania, noting that the longer she spent alone there, the more she recognised that every part of the natural world had a specific identity. She writes of her 'relationship' with the countryside around her:

> I named them and greeted them as friends. 'Good morning, Peak', I would say as I arrived there each morning; 'Hello, Stream' when I collected my water; 'Oh, Wind, for Heaven's sake, calm down' as it howled overhead.

In particular, she describes becoming intensely aware of 'the being-ness of trees'.

## The Wood Wide Web

Around 80% of Britain was originally woodland. As a result of agriculture and industry, that has fallen to around 13% today. Yet it seems many of us continue to harbour a desire to connect with trees. Their significance is not simply that they give us life by absorbing carbon dioxide and producing oxygen. They also connect us with ages past. Trees have been around for millions of years longer than we have, and many individual trees today are hundreds of years old. Their age, constancy, stability and strength help to put our own short lives into perspective. As such, they can hold a deep spiritual connection. Biologist Rupert Sheldrake suggests that 'they act as a bridge between the heavens and the Earth, their roots in the ground, connected to the rich life of the soil… with their branches reaching up to the sky and the sunlight'.

Before my pilgrimage, I often took the existence of trees for granted, walking blindly past even the most magnificent ones. During the journey, I began to perceive a deep connection with trees of differing sizes and ages. I would stop and place my hands on a particular tree, visualising the complex entwining of roots underneath. The roots would have been stretching out even further than the spectacular branches above, as they drew out water from the soil to feed the leaves canopying above me. This connection to trees is deep in the human psyche.

In 2018, the city council of Melbourne, Australia assigned email addresses to 70,000 trees, for people to report broken branches or other problems. To the council's surprise, they were inundated with thousands of love letters to individual trees from people who were making daily connections with their leafy neighbours. One young person wrote to a local elm tree: 'We don't have a lot in common, you being a tree and such, but I'm glad we're in this together.'

It was only after my walk that I familiarised myself with the work of Suzanne Simard and Peter Wohlleben, who explored how trees communicate with each other about dangers, health and needs via a network of roots and threads of microfungi. This has become affectionately known as the Wood Wide Web. According to Wohlleben, 'trees communicate by means of olfactory, visual, and electrical signals'. During my pilgrimage, I felt viscerally they were not only communicating with each other, but they were somehow also communicating with me.

One of highlights of the Pilgrim's Way is the ancient yew at St Digain's Church, Llangernyw, purported to be the oldest living tree in Europe and possibly the second oldest in the world. According to local tradition, the church is inhabited by an ancient spirit known as the *Angelystor* ('Recording Angel'), which, at midnight on Halloween and in a booming voice, is said to foretell the names of parishioners who will die in the following year. This ancient tree breaks at its base, forming various trunks, which allows pilgrims to climb into it. I stood inside its separated trunk, almost as if it were a wooden womb embracing its weary visitor. I felt a palpable, spiritual connection with that yew. Its gnarled branches and roots seemed to whisper echoes of the past, entwining my presence with the countless pilgrim souls who had stood there before me.

## Trees and our faith

Drawing on theologian Martin Buber's concept of I–Thou, Graham B. Usher suggests that, instead of viewing a tree as an 'it', a mere object separate from us, the Christian must encounter it as a 'thou', engaging with it in a spirit of respect, presence and connection. By employing Buber's philosophy he comes to an understanding of trees as 'responsive subjects and possessing agency, thus creating an interaction with us and with God'. After all, the biblical witness describes trees dancing, clapping and worshipping (for example, in Isaiah 55:12 and Ezekiel 17:24). As the psalmist wrote of the created order: 'They have no speech, they use no words; no sound is heard from them. Yet their voice goes out into all the earth, their words to the ends of the world' (Psalm 19:3–4). Thus, Usher writes, we can say we are able to 'hear' what trees 'say' to us. Early environmentalist John Muir even went as far as to claim that the tones of different species of trees are distinct and unique, each 'expressing itself in its own way – singing its own song, and making its own particular gestures'.

In Wales, a deep reverence for God's creation was at the heart of early Celtic Christianity's distinctive attitude to the cultic trees and groves of the pagans. On the continent, there are stories of early Christian missionaries preaching the gospel before taking out their axes and chopping down venerated trunks. In ancient Britain, though, churches were erected within druidic groves and next to the sacred trees of the pagan tradition, and pilgrimage sites developed out of these new holy places. Age-old trees and groves acquired a new Christianised meaning, with accompanying spiritual narratives, often centring around Celtic saints.

In fact, until the eleventh century, there is not a single record of a sacred oak, pine or yew being cut down in Britain and Ireland nor any decrees condemning their veneration. It seems, for the Celtic Christians, these sites were regarded as holding something of the primal quality of Eden and of the coming kingdom. As theologian Nikolai Berdyaev writes, beauty 'is either a memory of paradise or a prophecy of the transfigured world'.

On arriving at Bangor during my pilgrimage, I sat outside the impressive cathedral and ate my sandwiches in the 'Bible Garden', which is said to have within it every plant mentioned in the Bible. Perhaps such modern sacred groves, though, are not simply to be found in and around our places of worship. Rupert Sheldrake has suggested that the modern secular world has its own sacred groves in the guise of national parks. So, even the mountains of the national park of Eryri (Snowdonia) that I was traversing over could be held as one giant sacred grove. They certainly provide spiritual nourishment and inspiration for those whose eyes and hearts are open to this. As I immersed myself in the countryside, my own perspective began to shift. No longer did I see the natural world as something 'less-than-human'. Instead, I came to appreciate the truth in philosopher David Abram's insight that nature is, in fact, the 'more-than-human' world.

## The gift of place

The wonder I experienced during the pilgrimage, though, was not merely related to the beauty and sanctity of the natural world. Often it was rooted in specific geographic locations. Like the early Israelites who recalled and retold their salvation history, places connect us to our past and to the history of our forebears. They provide continuity and identity over many generations. They are a gift of God to humanity, even when they sometimes carry sorrowful and poignant memories. Barack Obama considered how, through place, the past can impact the present. After a visit to Stonehenge, he talked about ancient sites giving us perspective which lifts us from our daily anxieties and fears. Through spending time in these venerable places, he concludes, 'you're reminded that we are just part of this long chain, and we do our best with the little link of that chain that is allotted to us'.

Specific places can certainly engender a sense of awe and sanctity in us. Like Yahweh appearing to Moses at the burning bush (Exodus 3:5), the transcendent breaks through in these places, touching our being and demanding a response. Just as Moses removed his shoes, we will often respond with reverence, humility and wonder. George MacLeod, a Scottish minister who restored the monastery on Iona in 1938, coined the phrase 'thin places' to describe those places where the membrane between earth and heaven, between this world and the next, seems slight.

The ancient Celts undoubtedly believed certain places to be holy, with early Welsh Christians holding that places root us in a greater power. Many continue to affirm the immanence and presence of God in these places. I felt that ancient holy sites on the Pilgrim's Way, from pre-Christian megaliths to churches and holy wells, seemed to lift me upwards, beyond the worries, limitations and pain I was enduring. God's glory is no doubt written on every part of his creation, but in some places he writes in capital letters.

Rupert Sheldrake has posited that the sense of connection and wonder we feel in specific locations can be explored scientifically. He suggests that places have a kind of memory of the past. He terms this concept 'morphic resonance' – the idea that places have a memory that we can feel and to which we contribute. Thus, Carl Jung's concept of the collective unconscious, the distilled inherited memory of humankind, can be related to geographical places. History, therefore, becomes like energy waves that we can pick up and experience, as if we are tuning to the correct station on a radio. In particular, in so-called 'holy' places, where people have long prayed or worshipped, we come into resonance with the powerful stimuli those have experienced in the past. 'If pilgrims to a holy place have been inspired, uplifted or healed,' Sheldrake writes, 'there we are more likely to have similar experiences of spiritual connection.'

Most of us can see traces of the past on our bodies. For me, there is a small scar on my forehead where my brother accidentally hit me with a can of coke almost 40 years ago and a large scar on my back where the titanium bolt was inserted to stabilise my spine. But our minds and emotions also bear imprints of the journeys we have taken, the places we have visited and the people who have touched our lives. Sheldrake is suggesting that geographical places are likewise inhabited by such imprints of the past. These are more than the physical, historical scars. Rather, he argues that places hold something tangible of the events and people of the past. The past and present are inextricably bound in these places, as if there is an invisible thread, gently pulling us backwards to the past.

## Profound connections of time and place

Descending into the valley of Bontnewydd in Clwyd, near the River Elwy, was one of the most awe-inspiring and humbling experiences of my pilgrimage. I had struggled down an exceptionally steep road to the village, limping down due to pain in my knee. Yet when I arrived at the floor of the valley, there was something about this small hamlet that stopped me in my tracks – something that I cannot easily put into words. The place spoke to me with a peace and serenity that I have rarely experienced. I knew immediately that there was something 'special', even holy, about the place. As it happens, Bontnewydd has a long and ancient history. Some of the earliest known remains of Neanderthals in Britain were found in this valley. Dated to 230,000 years ago, the bones were of an eleven-year-old boy and at least four other Neanderthal adults. As I stood, I could feel the transhistorical power of this place, a special connection beyond linear time, a seem-ingly personal connection with those who, down the millennia, had flourished and struggled in this ancient valley.

There were other such moments during the pilgrimage, albeit not always as tangible, when I felt a similar connection. Often it was in places with a visible or invisible imprint of its past, but at other times it was in the resplendent beauty of the natural world. Sometimes, it was a combination of both. French philosopher Maurice Merleau-Ponty suggests there is a continual and unique interchange between our individual bodies and the world around us and, in recognising this, we can achieve a deeper awareness of ourselves and our surroundings. I have never felt this interchange as tangibly as in moments of awe and wonder on this pilgrimage – sitting eating my lunch staring out at seals bobbing in the waves, sheltering in an ancient chapel while rain lashed against the outside walls, lying exhausted on a remote hillside as the spring sun warmed my face, and even resting in the revitalis-ing salt-baths that I took at the end of each day. My journey led me to touch something universal and profound through the language of God's created world. I was experiencing the 'sublime' which writers in the 18th and 19th centuries mused about. As English dramatist John

Dennis, the person who originally coined the word 'sublime', wrote after walking in the Alps: 'The sense of all this produc'd different motions in me, *viz.* a delightful Horrour, a terrible Joy, and at the same time, that I was infinitely pleas'd, I trembled.'

## JOURNEY TWO: THROUGH INJURY AND DARKNESS

## A pilgrimage mindset

After returning home from my pilgrimage and beginning the long road to recovery, I found my encounters with nature had shifted. They felt different, but no less profound. Despite the physical pain and mental turmoil that weighed me down, God's presence in the natural world found ways to break through. Even as I lay on my sofa for what felt like endless hours, there were moments when my connection to creation ran as deep as ever. Yet, in the very early days of recovery, burdened by injury and uncertainty, recognising God's light amid the shadows of my struggle was anything but easy.

Each time she left the Tanzanian jungle for her lecture tours of US and UK cities, primatologist Jane Goodall described how distant she felt from her life-giving faith. I had experienced God in a profound way on my pilgrimage and so, in finding myself facing acute pain upon my return, I also initially felt spiritually bereft. When I first returned home from pilgrimage, my mind, tangled in anxious thoughts, made it hard to see or feel God's wonder. It was as if a fog had settled over my heart, dimming the light I once recognised so easily.

Goodall writes that she eventually learnt to 'keep the peace of the forest within' on her lecture tours. While it was not an easy task while facing pain and anxiety, I also learnt to draw on my memories of the walk and I was able to gain strength from the beauty that had somehow remained in me. In the final verse of Wordsworth's 'I wandered lonely as a cloud', the poet lies back on his couch, in a pensive mood, and is returned in a vivid way to the walk that he trod and the 'host of golden daffodils' that he had seen. This lifts his heart and brings him joy:

> *They flash upon that inward eye*
> *Which is the bliss of solitude;*
> *And then my heart with pleasure fills,*
> *And dances with the daffodils.*

Echoes of the transcendent experiences during my first pilgrimage fed into my second pilgrimage, and in time, these memories were able to sustain and inspire me in the midst of the pain.

At those times when I found myself wrestling with a heavy mental fog that clouded my memories, I would force myself to step outside, taking short walks despite the pain, determined to reclaim a sense of movement and connection. Slowly but surely a pilgrimage mindset started to take precedence over the anxiety. In fact, pain itself allowed an appreciation of God's creation in a unique way. 'I will love the light for it shows me the way,' wrote Og Mandino, 'yet I will endure the darkness because it shows me the stars'. And so, just as I had delighted in rocks, streams and trees on my walk, I began to appreciate familiar objects that were all around me in the house, outside the window or on the short walks I undertook. I began to experience things I had known for nearly half a century in a refreshingly different light.

## Paradise city

Our back garden particularly became a haven to me, as I paced around, trying desperately to relieve the pain through movement. The book of Genesis paints paradise as a garden, a place where humans, plants and animals exist in perfect harmony with their creator. In a small but meaningful way, our own gardens, our local parks and our neighbourhood allotments echo that original balance, offering a glimpse of the beauty and order that was lost after the fall. I would even discard the layers of cotton and rubber between my body and the ground by taking off my shoes and socks to walk around the garden barefoot, connecting directly with God's earth. Feeling the grass beneath my toes, brushing against the soles of my feet, awakened something precious and uplifting within me. Each blade tickled my nerves and reflex points, a simple yet deeply moving sensation. But the experience was even more poignant given that, due to nerve damage from my back injury, much of the feeling in one foot had faded.

Before long, as I grew stronger, short walks around the city lake that our house overlooked brought much-needed solace. I realised I had not fully appreciated the lake when we had moved there five years earlier. It had not seemed wild or untamed enough for someone hailing from Eryri. Now, though, it became my sanctuary. The lake itself remained unchanged, but my injury had reshaped my relationship with it entirely. As Immanuel Kant wrote: 'What in truth is sublime must be sought in the mind of the judging subject, and not in those objects of nature which give rise to the mood.'

During these short lake walks, I entered moments when time and space seemed inconsequential and my ego was relinquished. In those moments, I was fully immersed in my surroundings, free from the need to cling to control. This sense of what social psychologist Mihaly Csikszentmihalyi calls 'flow' can emerge in many ways, whether through cooking, painting, kneading dough or even playing darts, snooker or bowls. But out in the countryside, it often comes more easily. The worries that usually chatter away in our minds soften into silence, making space for a deep and settling calm. Nineteenth-century psychologist William James described moments when we find ourselves 'most deeply and intensely active and alive'. This is, he claimed, when each of us will find the 'real me'.

Even when my pain was too intense to leave my red sofa, the wonder of nature still broke through. I would be lifted by watching the green woodpecker on the trees across from my house, with its distinctive yaffle call, and the flock of long-tailed tits that would visit the magnolia tree outside my bedroom window. These small energetic birds, described as 'flying teaspoons' in some areas of the country and 'feathered lollipops' by the naturalist Emma Mitchell, became a healing treasure for me. I even began to feel a deep connection with the magnolia tree itself. In recent years, we have taken it upon ourselves to protect trees with preservation orders and forest maintenance. Mayhew-Smith points out that this is an 'inversion of our troubled hierarchy in the natural world'. Historically, it was trees, not least sacred and venerated ones, which were seen as protecting us, rather than the other way round. In physical and emotional pain, I felt as if this magnolia tree was somehow feeling my predicament and watching over me.

## Thin moments

In his seminal study *A Secular Age*, Charles Taylor compares the pre-Reformation world, where physical objects, people and places held spiritual power, to the post-Reformation world, where the world started to become disenchanted. So, people became trapped in their minds and the world on the outside lost its significance. During my journey of recovery, I soon realised my mind held few answers. In fact, I found myself incarcerated in anxiety and melancholy. Freedom involved immersing myself in God's creation and opening my eyes, ears and heart to the ethereal dimension of the natural world. When early European explorers introduced glass to remote tribes on distant islands, it is said that it was so alien to them that they could only focus on the glass itself – they could see the glass, but they could not see through it. Our call as Christians is not to be bound up in our thoughts and feelings, but neither is it simply to focus on the world around us. Instead, we see beyond and through the material world and recognise the kingdom of God all around us.

Rather than the 'thin places' of my Celtic ancestors, my experience during my journey of recovery was of 'thin moments'. These were moments when another dimension seemed to break through my daily grind. Charles Foster uses the analogy of the wardrobe in C.S. Lewis' Narnia chronicles to describe such fleeting moments: 'You can feel the fur coats on your cheek, and there are moments when you can almost feel a snowflake on your nose, or the brush of a pine tree.' Lewis himself noted that times of wonder are even more vivid when we are suffering. He describes our hearts being lifted by stabs of joy. These are not long lasting, nor are they stable and secure. But, in and through them, we glimpse something greater, something eternal. They are joyous moments, when we experience green shoots in our desert journeys. As Janet Erskine Stuart noted: 'Joy is not the absence of suffering but the presence of God.'

Compared to the intensity of my North Wales journey, connection with the natural world was less intense and less frequent during my second pilgrimage. Yet when those moments did come, they came suddenly and unexpectedly, as when the blue flash of a kingfisher dazzled me as I walked round the lake. Occasionally, moments of wonder were more purposeful and arranged. On rainy days, I would lie on the sofa in my back room and open our patio doors. Listening and watching the pattering of drops on the back garden, I felt enclosed and safe. My frustration and anxiety dissipated and I felt uplifted and at peace.

As I was unable to sit or stand for any length of time, the spiritual sustenance of long church services was not possible. As well as being visited by kindly priests for home Communion, I was able to recreate a faint glimmer of the connection of the Eucharist service in an unusual manner. Each Sunday I would take my breakfast to the side of the lake and share crumbs with the ducks and geese. I reminded myself that, in some small way, this echoed biblical moments of spiritual connection through provision and sustenance, such as the exchange of food between Elijah and the ravens in 1 Kings 17 and the last supper in the gospel narratives. While this could never replace my need for the Eucharistic sacrament, sharing my bread with such unconventional company stirred something deeply spiritual within me. After all, the very word 'company' comes from the Latin *cum pane*, meaning 'with bread'. And so in this simple act each week, there was a glimpse of what Kierkegaard called a 'consciousness of eternity', a sense of the divine that, he observed, shines most brightly in times of turmoil and suffering.

# ON OUR JOURNEYS

## Well-being and nature

Recent research reveals that immersing ourselves in the natural world during our journeys actively enhances our emotional and physical well-being. Biologist Edward O. Wilson attributes this to our deep-rooted instinct to connect with the natural world, a legacy of our ancestors who lived as hunter-gatherers, intimately tied to the land. He terms this *biophilia*. Yet, increasingly, we are alienated from our natural environments and find ourselves immersed more frequently in the digital world. Richard Louv created the term 'nature-deficit disorder' to describe the consequences of this disconnect on the health of individuals and on the social fabric. He found that young children, for example, identified far more readily with cartoon characters than the trees, birds or animals in their locality. Even more startlingly, British prison inmates spend more time outdoors than 75% of children.

The lack of connection with the countryside, however, is affecting not only young people. All of us are increasingly alienated from nature and our present mental health crises may stem in no small part from that. Scientists have discovered that various physiological and neurological changes take place when we are outdoors in the presence of fauna and flora. Nature can alter the balance of the neurotransmitters in our brains, providing us with doses of mind-shifting brain chemicals. Research from various universities, from Exeter to Madrid, has shown that not only can time spent outdoors help recovery from depression and anxiety, but simply gazing at the natural world through a living room window can considerably benefit the mind and lift our mood.

As Jesus understood when he spoke of the birds of the air and the lilies of the field (Matthew 6:25–29), nature has a way of shifting our perspective. It loosens the grip of life's details, allowing us to step back and see the bigger picture with greater clarity. Kierkegaard described himself 'empowered to perceive things differently' through the 'deep but quietly earnest song' of the sea, the 'congregational hymns of praise' of the birds and the 'call to prayer' of nature. Likewise, Iris Murdoch, in her book *The Sovereignty of Good*, recalls being in an anxious state, brooding on a difficulty she faced. She looked out of her window and noticed a hovering kestrel. As she stood, entranced by the bird of prey, she describes how her mindset slowly altered. 'There is nothing now but kestrel,' she concludes, 'and when I return to thinking of the other matter it seems less important.'

On my North Wales pilgrimage, as I walked on the cliffs, gazing out on the rolling sea, I felt as if I was a world away from my everyday frantic busyness. Marine biologist Wallace Nichols suggests that gazing out to sea gives us a break from the continual visual stimuli we receive in our daily lives. But a similar sabbatical for the mind can be embraced in whatever environment is local to us. Near our home is a small patch of woodland, no more than the size of a football pitch. During my recovery, I spent time in it, embracing the Japanese practice of 'forest bathing' (*shinrin-yoku*), allowing this woodland area to calm and comfort my mind. Researchers at Chiba University in Japan have shown that such a simple therapy is able to strengthen the immune system, reduce stress, and lower cholesterol and blood pressure. The practice is hugely popular in Japan, with 48 officially designated bathing forests. As naturalist Emma Mitchell puts it: 'It is no more unusual to seek out trees and plants when feeling unwell in Japan than it is to nip to the chemist for some ibuprofen in the UK.'

# Connecting with the creator God

For Christians, our connection with the natural world is not simply because it aids our mental health or that we find it aesthetically pleasing. Rather, there is something of the wonder of nature that connects us to our creator God. The spiritual experience is far more complex than simply being calmed or inspired through nature. Instead, the sublime lifts us to a 'state of elevation', as the 19th-century philosopher Schopenhauer put it. This points to something beyond nature. It allows us to abandon ourselves to a God who offers freedom from the worries and desires that incarcerate us. Some connect through great and grand moments, whether gazing at the stars above or taking in a breathtaking sunset. But, for others, the sublime is found in the simplicity of a peaceful walk in the park, a sudden downpour as we put out the washing on the line, or a surprise visit of a robin on our window ledge.

The feelings of awe and wonder that break through at these times are embedded deep in our evolutionary past. Even the chimpanzees in the Gombe jungle in Tanzania were described by Jane Goodall as having 'feelings akin to awe'. They often performed a magnificent dance at the breathtaking Kakombe valley waterfall, which she suggested was like basic religious worship. This was, she wrote, 'generated by the mystery of water; water that seems alive, always rushing past yet never going, always the same yet ever different'.

Celtic Christianity recognised the divine in our own moments of connection with the natural world. By now, apart from the occasional 'forest church' service, our worship is largely stuck behind the four walls of our church buildings. In Niall Griffiths' novel *Grits*, set in Aberystwyth, Liam claims that, in its early days, the church 'startud to build places whur we could supposedly meet God an ignore all the places whur ee actually is'. The ancient British texts that have survived certainly paint a vivid picture of early Celtic Christians interacting with the God of the birds, animals and trees, as they lived as hermits on remote islands, faced demons on the top of mountains, and even prayed naked in freezing rivers. Their lives, and indeed their faith, was steeped in the natural world.

The Celtic attitude to nature, rooted in scripture, arose from a desire to show that creation flowed from the Christian God and not from pagan gods. The early Celtic Christians were approaching mission in a pioneering manner. In encountering a Celtic paganism rooted in the local, non-urbanised environment, Christianity had to adapt its message and its outreach. Much of the philosophical theology of the Greek and Roman world did not resonate with the Celtic people. Instead, like the apostle Paul modifying his preaching to the market-place in Athens, the church adapted by rooting itself in the world of flora, fauna and the rugged, unruly terrains of the sea and mountains. As Nick Mayhew-Smith points out, for the early Celtic Christians nature contained the 'rudimentary infrastructure of a church': the rhythm of the tides echoed the rhythm of praise, large rocks provided platforms for preaching and sacred trees offered shelter to hold worship.

Early Welsh Christianity was, then, distinctive in affirming an immanent God, as close and present as the natural world. Over time, a quiet but profound separation unfolded between the spiritual and the natural world. Nick Mayhew-Smith describes this as the 'desacralization of nature'. As a result, much of the awe and reverence that once came so naturally to past generations faded. Belden Lane describes this shift as a 'modern hermeneutics of suspicion' which dismisses, and sometimes ridicules, the idea of finding the sacred in nature. He concludes that 'the path has been lost that goes back to the burning bush'.

## Traces of the Trinity

While it is tempting to consider these early Celtic attitudes as archaic and primitive, they chime with recent scientific thinking. A number of prominent scientists and philosophers, including Galen Strawson and Thomas Nagel, have suggested that all atoms and molecules have a consciousness of sorts. Panpsychism suggests we have an innate connection with the natural world due to the presence of an 'extended mind', 'nonlocal mind' or 'entangled mind'. Rupert Sheldrake suggests that this universal consciousness is not merely the root of our own complex minds, but is an echo of God's ultimate consciousness. In other words, the consciousness that shapes the universe flows through all of nature and both animal and human minds are ultimately derived from it. So, in this sense, God is both beyond the natural world and deeply present within it. Every part of creation exists within him and shares in his being (Colossians 1:16–17).

This idea connects to a theological approach that recognises 'traces of the Trinity' (*Vestigia Trinitatis*) woven into our human experiences. As Peter J. Leithart puts it, the Trinity can be glimpsed 'under every stone and in every sunset and in the face of every stranger'. Just as the three persons of the Trinity dwell within one another, they also dwell within all of reality, including the natural world. When we encounter moments of beauty in nature, we are witnessing the Trinity's presence, like a divine dance moving through the world around us.

As I recovered from my back injury, in physical and emotional pain and unable to experience the wildness of my earlier pilgrimage, my eyes were opened to the dance of the Trinity in far more basic ways – through visitors to my bird table, rustling leaves on the trees outside my window, short walks in my local park, roses in the garden, and rain beating against the patio doors. In reflecting on her time in Auschwitz, psychologist Edith Eger suggested that the one thing we are left with in any suffering is the choice of how we respond to it. In this sense, she claims we are left with a stark choice: 'To become bitter in our grief and fear. Hostile. Paralyzed. Or to hold on to the childlike part of us, the lively and curious part, the part that is innocent.'

When we are in the midst of life's storms, embracing that childlike capacity for awe and wonder is not easy. But it can serve as an anchor, grounding us in something greater than our struggles and reminding us that hope and meaning exist, even in life's darkest moments. In his poem 'Counterpoint', R.S. Thomas suggests that it sometimes seems as if God, the bride at the wedding, is playing hide and seek with us. Yet, in those moments, when the bride herself seems invisible, Thomas urges us to recognise the sparkling specks of confetti that are scattered all around. When we connect with the natural world, that confetti is at its most vivid and beautiful.

## TIME TO REFLECT

- How do you most intuitively connect with the awe and wonder of the natural world?

- In what ways does God speak to you through creation?

- In the days ahead, consider how you might make space to rest in the beauty of nature – whether walking in the countryside, sitting in a garden or park, or simply pausing to notice the world outside your window.

# 3

# Signs

---

*I have now lived a hundred and nine winters in this world and have never yet met any such thing as Luck.*

Hermit to Aravis in C.S. Lewis, *The Horse and His Boy*

*There is a voice that doesn't use words. Listen.*

Rumi, poet

## JOURNEY ONE: PILGRIM'S WAY

### Waymarkers on our journeys

Signposts were a lifeline during my North Wales pilgrimage. In fact, weeks after returning home, I still found myself dreaming about those small, white, circular waymarkers that had guided me through the journey. I strayed from the pilgrim path on countless occasions, but without waymarkers I would have spent many more hours aimlessly wandering the rugged Eryri (Snowdonia) countryside, lost and frustrated.

Yet these markers were more than just practical; they were symbols of direction and reassurance, quietly pointing the way forward. There was a thrill in searching for them and a small triumph in finding them, as many were hidden by greenery or damaged through wear and tear. They also needed to be read correctly, as it was often a matter of interpretation which way the arrow was pointing! Each one demanded careful attention, reminding me that staying on the right path was never about mindlessly following signs, but required discernment, patience and trust.

Just as waymarkers guide pilgrims along their route, Christians have long held that God provides guideposts for our lives. Though he exists beyond time and space, he still works within them to lead and sustain us, actively engaging in the details of our daily journeys. Sometimes, God's signs are bold, unmistakable moments of clarity that awaken us to new possibilities. More often, they are quiet and subtle, as his 'still small voice' (1 Kings 19:12, RSV) gently nudges us. A waymarker for a pilgrim is no more or less important because of its size or prominence. Likewise, whether loud or subtle, whether through startling, sudden awakenings or quieter, long-term realisations, God's voice holds meaning. Our call is to open ourselves to these moments breaking into our lives and to the possibility that a personal God is behind them. When we do, we create space to reflect on their meaning, allowing these divine stirrings to shape our journeys.

Psychotherapist David Richo calls these signs 'phenomenons of grace' and describes them stemming from a power and presence beyond us. So, God reaches into our lives in unexpected ways, whether through moments of intuition, emotions, dreams, creativity and encounters. Perhaps the most striking way he speaks is through meaningful coincidences. The materialist worldview might dismiss these as mere random events, the inevitable workings of probability that we casually label as 'luck' or 'chance'. Christians, though, see something deeper at play. These are moments when God's will intersects with our lives in unexpected ways. Through these occurrences, he offers opportunities, guidance and warnings.

## Seeing signs and wonders

Recognising the routine revelation of God's will and presence in our daily lives is far from superstition. Instead, an awareness of God as a gentle companion, guiding us and inspiring us, is firmly rooted in scripture. The biblical God is an intimate God, active in our lives and in history. After all, the Bible is rich with both subtle and explicit reminders of this. Expressions like 'the hand of God', 'the face of God', 'the blessing', 'the kingdom', and 'the plan of God' appear frequently, emphasising his continual involvement. Furthermore, both the Old and New Testament are records of people responding to God's call, with new possibilities emerging from that dialogue. The prophet Isaiah (30:21) captures this beautifully: 'Whether you turn to the right or to the left, your ears will hear a voice behind you, saying, "This is the way; walk in it."' Even when biblical figures stray or make poor choices, God provides new redemptive paths. Jonah, for example, runs from God's call, only to be redirected back to his mission, highlighting God's persistence, guidance and grace.

Sometimes our secular mindset finds this concept hard to comprehend and accept. Even within Christian theological circles, suspicion of the concept of God's providence began to grow from the 19th century, not least because of the embarrassment of 'God-led' colonisation and imperialism. Yet, in recent years there has been a gradual return to affirming the biblical reality of a caring, preserving and guiding God. This shift reflects a growing desire to understand God's providence not as a tool of power, but as a source of hope, guidance and compassion in an uncertain world.

In the reaction of the onlookers to the *semeia* ('signs') of John's gospel, though, lies a warning about our own attitudes to moments of guidance and grace. John's seven signs are wondrous miracles which may have originated in a separate, earlier document known as the 'signs source'. They are hugely important to the gospel writer – they show who Jesus really is and what he reveals to us. Yet, it was only people whose eyes were open to noticing God's will amid the ordinariness of their lives who fully recognised the significance of these spiritual moments. Many were so preoccupied with satiating their hunger at the feeding of the 5,000 that they missed the wonder of that sign, just as many at the wedding in Cana, when Jesus changed water to wine, were too busy making merry to recognise that wonder. 'Unless you people *see* signs and wonders… you will never believe', Jesus said (John 4:48, my emphasis). It therefore takes a deep sense of awareness and attentiveness to recognise the signs all around us. When we do, something extraordinary happens – our outward and inward journeys beautifully converge.

So, our call is to open our eyes, ears and hearts to notice God's kingdom, the subtle but profound manifestations of his will, breaking through. In the hustle and noise of our busy lives, it is all too easy to overlook these fleeting glimpses of heaven in the everyday. As psychologist Carl Jung observed: 'Modern people don't see God because they don't look low enough.' To encounter him, we must pause and pay attention, reflecting on the meaning behind everyday situations and the significance of coincidences, however small they may seem. At the core of our Christian journey is the discovery of profound spiritual meaning woven into the threads of daily life. The seemingly ordinary is touched by holiness, and the mundane becomes a part of God's loving plan.

## Pilgrimage signs

The Medieval pilgrims who walked the Pilgrim's Way would have used the phrase *unus mundus* ('one world') to refer to the unity of matter and spirit which are continually interacting. During my own pilgrimage, I began to notice signs in which that unity was becoming manifest, signs that reassured me of God's presence on my journey. The cadences of God's voice were sometimes subtle and sometimes striking. The coincidences I encountered on my journey took on a profound significance. As such, my pilgrimage became a series of 'God winks', those subtle, yet powerful, moments when God's presence reassures and inspires us, often through the mystery of coincidence.

About halfway through my 15-mile walk on the second day of my pilgrimage, I stopped at Pantasaph Friary, a Franciscan friary. There I bumped into an old student of mine from many years back. As we sat and talked about the coincidence of us both visiting the café on the same day, my eyes were drawn to an elderly friar knitting silently, a steaming cup of tea by his side. Intrigued, I struck up a conversation with this contemplative knitter. He was warm and charming, and, as I stood to leave, he promised to pray for my journey. We exchanged names, and he introduced himself as Fr Francis.

The name stopped me in my tracks. I told him that, coincidentally, a 'Fr Francis' had profoundly shaped my faith journey as a teenager. I had once attended a concert of his where he played both religious and secular songs on the guitar and even performed faith-filled stand-up comedy. That evening sparked something in me – a passion for exploring religious themes in secular music and a deep appreciation for the connection between humour and faith. I had even bought a tape of the concert, which was played so often it eventually wore out. The friar listened intently, a twinkle in his eye. Then he leaned in and, with a knowing smile, said, 'Young man, I am that very Fr Francis – or as they used to call me, the "singing friar"!' I was stunned and over-joyed. It was as if the years had folded in on themselves, giving me the chance to thank him for the influence he had on my life. And from his heartfelt reaction, I could tell that knowing his work had made a difference meant the world to him.

At other points on the pilgrimage, these moments of coincidence and connection came from an unexpected source. As I travelled across Eryri, I met an avid metal detectorist who was reminiscent of a character on BBC's hit comedy *Detectorists*. A lively and chatty character, he enthusiastically described his treasure-hunting hobby before asking me why I was walking through a random field outside Bangor. No sooner had I started to explain about my pilgrimage, he was suddenly more animated than ever. He explained he had coincidentally found a rather special object in that field only a week earlier. He whipped out his phone and showed me a photograph of an ancient pendant shaped as a scallop shell, used by pilgrims as an emblem of their journey since as early as the Middle Ages. This detectorist had exca-vated a centuries-old pilgrim's pendant, replete with a hole on the top, where string would have threaded through so the shell could be worn around the neck. I was excited to show him my own pilgrim's shell, which had been given to me by my mother as I embarked on my walk and which I carried in my pocket for the whole 140 miles. It was a staggering thought that many hundreds of years ago a pilgrim, just like me, would have been walking on that same field when he lost his scallop shell pendant. This connection led to an in-depth discussion about theology and faith with the treasure hunter. I left that field with the strong sense that the Spirit had inspired both the coincidence and the subsequent conversation.

Another meaningful 'sign' during my pilgrimage, which uplifted me and brought me comfort during a particular difficult leg of the journey, was an even more striking coincidence. After almost a week walking, I was tired, drained and missing my family, who were a four-hour drive away in Cardiff. I had walked around 15 miles that day, battling excruciating knee pain and strengthened mostly with dried raisins and bottled water. I walked into St Martin's Church in Eglwysbach, my final stop for that day, to get the stamp on my pilgrim's passport. As I walked in, I was astonished to see my wife and daughter smiling back at me. But this was no hallucination. They were, in fact, on the front cover of a magazine. The publication, which was almost ten years old, had an article in it about the comfort and strength that God gave to my wife through loss and grief she had faced in her life. The coincidence was striking – this fading magazine was the only one in this church and it was being displayed prominently. I spent some time in prayer for my family and went on my way, ready for my 15 miles on the next day, uplifted and strengthened by this strange and magnificent moment of connection.

## Breaking through the frame

Theologian Charles Taylor describes how we, in the 21st century, are trapped within an 'immanent frame'. It is as if we are living in a picture in an art gallery, enclosed in a thick, immovable frame. The prevalent materialist worldview cannot see beyond or outside that frame and insists that the picture inside the frame is all there is. Faith dares us to see beyond this rigid boundary, to notice the cracks in the frame that hint at something greater. My pilgrimage became a journey of seeing beyond that constraining frame. Each step opened me to a strange new world, one brimming with wonder, beauty and delight. Alongside these daily blessings, I began to experience such uncanny, uplifting coincidences. They were moments that felt like shafts of light breaking through the cracks, revealing glimpses of something far more profound than that offered by the picture within the frame. They pointed to the extraordinary, inviting me to step beyond the limits and encounter the divine in life-affirming and inspiring ways.

## JOURNEY TWO: THROUGH INJURY AND DARKNESS

## Meaningful coincidences

Charles Foster writes that 'when you walk as a pilgrim along a kingdom road, where every step is a prayer, coincidences happen'. It is in the moments when the path feels darkest and the struggle is most raw that the light of strange and breathtaking connections shines brightest. Languishing and listening, after all, go hand in hand. When we thirst, when our souls ache for meaning and renewal, we become more open to the quenching fulfilment of the living water that only God can provide.

After a particularly dark few days during my recovery, I lay in my bedroom in excruciating pain. My mind started dwelling on how bleak the future seemed. I looked outside with tears in my eyes and there, on the telephone wire, staring directly at me, was a goldfinch. It had been many months, if not years, since I had seen one of these beautiful birds. For a moment, my worries faded and I was entranced by this heavenly visitor. As it flew away, I reached down for my iPad and, for some reason, was prompted to search: 'What is the meaning of seeing a goldfinch?' I was faced with dozens of classical paintings of Jesus holding goldfinches. It turns out that there has long been a link between faith and goldfinches. It was even believed that the bird's red face was a result of it trying to remove Jesus' crown of thorns. I then read that, down the years, the goldfinch has been related to Christian healing. There I was, languishing physically and mentally, and I was visited by a traditional symbol of healing.

Received scientific 'wisdom' may well dismiss this event as random coincidence. A spiritual reading of the situation would be ridiculed as a desperate grasping for hope. Yet in her autobiography, Jane Goodall questions the contemporary inclination towards viewing the world as simply a place of blind chance and fate. She describes how two children in different parts of the world – her son in an English boarding school and a family friend with Down syndrome in Tanzania – both had vivid dreams about her husband dying on the very night that he passed away. She claims it is far too easy for a sceptical, reductionist world to dismiss these experiences as psychological reactions or coincidental dreams. Perhaps, she concludes, science simply 'does not have appropriate tools for the dissection of the spirit'. It is certainly true that such meaningful coincidences can introduce us to a world beyond rational scientism, but such beliefs should not therefore be regarded as anti-scientific or unscientific. In fact, there has been revealing scientific research on meaningful coincidences.

The most prominent scientist to endorse and develop such thinking was the psychiatrist Carl Jung, who saw profound significance in coincidences, which he regarded as beyond the probability of chance. He described such 'synchronistic' events as 'acts of creation in time' which are 'an ever-present reality for those who have eyes to see'. The lives of his patients become a deep quarry for him to mine in his search for synchronistic evidence. He famously described a young woman who was resistant to his treatment until she had a dream about a golden scarab beetle. On telling Jung about this dream, they heard tapping on the office window. Jung opened the window and a scarab beetle flew into the room. Jung writes that this synchronistic event led to a sea change in the patient's attitude and opened her to life's spiritual dimension.

During my journey of recovery, the simple visit from a goldfinch became my own scarab-beetle moment. In a time of great turmoil, its presence brought me a deep sense of comfort and hope. It even continued to nourish me spiritually years later. I have often shared this story in my talks and writing, and, to my surprise, it has inspired others in their own spiritual journeys. I have even received messages from people moved by the story, some sharing their own meaningful encounters with goldfinches, each one a reminder of the mysterious ways God's presence reassures and inspires.

## The science of signs

Jung was certainly not alone among great thinkers who embraced the possibility of a mysterious force at work in our daily lives, imposing order on the apparent chaos around us. Philosophers such as Hegel, Schopenhauer and Von Schiller and scientists like the renowned biologist Paul Kammerer have maintained that chains of circumstances are linked in profound ways. Jung's thinking was later inspired by quantum mechanics, which he saw as proof that the universe did not act and react as a machine. Nobel-Prize-winning quantum physicist Wolfgang Pauli, who worked closely with Jung, described 'visible traces of untraceable principles' in referring to distinct events that are related despite no direct cause-and-effect link. Thus, Jung was able to refer to 'acausal connecting principles' in recognising connections through meaning, rather than by cause and effect.

There were certainly times in the 20th century when the relationship between mainstream science and spirituality was intimate. Even Einstein wrote that 'coincidence is God's way of remaining anonymous'.

By the end of the century, though, the separation between science and faith had widened. While working as lead university chaplain of an interfaith team some years ago, I officiated at annual services in the laboratory where first-year medical students would dissect cadavers of those who had donated their bodies to science. After a number of years of profoundly moving and much-appreciated services, a new professor was appointed who announced that the spiritual element of this service was to be discontinued, including my own role in the service. This reflects the general attitude of a certain element of the scientific community to things 'spiritual'.

Still, there continues to be branches of science which can aid us in understanding meaningful coincidences. Systems science, for example, holds that the macro and the micro are intimately related, as 'the all is in the small' and the 'small is in the all'. Thus, if Christians hold that God is present in the macro system (the universe), then his relationship with the micro system (our personal lives) can be affirmed. As American psychiatrist Gary E. Schwartz puts it, systems science opens the door to belief in a power that is 'Guiding. Organising. Designing. (G.O.D.)'.

Contemporary theology has engaged fruitfully with such concepts. The theological approach of 'open theism', in particular, has fostered a conversation between the biblical tradition and recent scientific and philosophical developments. By doing so, it has grasped something of the practicalities of how God's signs and guidance could work. Open theists hold that our future is still, in some way, undecided. To state that God is omniscient (all-knowing) does not, therefore, mean he determines the result of our choices. Rather, it refers to the infinite possibilities of our futures and it allows us the choice of how we live out those possibilities. Thus, we can still affirm that God's knowledge is perfect. 'God knows the future exactly as it is,' writes theologian Richard Rice, 'as partly definite and partly indefinite.'

This concept allows us to embrace the idea that, in every choice and in every decision, we are presented with an infinite number of pathways. While God nudges and guides us towards the most loving and compassionate path, we are at liberty to reject or ignore his guidance. After all, love cannot be coerced, but must be freely chosen. If we do reject the more loving path through a particular action or decision we make, though, we are soon then left with another limitless set of pathways. Again, God wills us to choose the most loving path in this new set of choices, and so on.

In the fourth volume of C.S. Lewis' Narnia series, *Prince Caspian*, Lucy notices signs that Aslan gives to guide her group on their journey to defeat the evil King Miraz. The rest of her group, though, refuse to believe she is being directed, so they ignore her and choose another path. Aslan, though, continues to appear to Lucy and eventually brings about his purposes. Likewise, in our own lives, God is present, flowing through all things, guiding us and presenting us with fresh possibilities to live out his love. Once we accept or reject a certain pathway, God ensures that other routes are revealed. In exploring God's providence, theologians Logan Williams and Haley Goranson Jacob have suggested a fresh understanding of the apostle Paul's oft-quoted assertion that 'in all things God works for the good of those who love him' (Romans 8:28). They have maintained that a closer translation to the original Greek would be 'God co-works, with those who love God, all things for good'. In other words, through his signs, God guides and leads us to embrace circumstances in line with his loving will.

# ON OUR JOURNEYS

## The wonderful dance

The concept of a God who knows every detail of our lives can feel enslaving and disempowering, especially for those experiencing the trauma of regret for actions taken or not taken. But embracing this new way of viewing God's omniscience is liberating. During my journey of recovery, I spent many months in turmoil, asking why God did not shield me from my injury by preventing me from going on my North Wales pilgrimage. Engaging with this fresh concept of God's guidance allowed me to reject the 'what ifs' that were keeping me in bondage. However far we wander away from our pilgrimage trail, there is freedom in recognising the next choice of path is the only one that now matters.

While training for ministry at Oxford, I taught Ceroc, a form of modern jive, to supplement my income. It was particularly appealing because, within a basic set structure, there is so much freedom. There are, for example, no formal or complex dance steps to learn. Instead, there are a set of routines for the upper half of the body, while the lower half is free for improvisation and spontaneity. Noticing and responding to synchronistic moments in our lives is like being part of a wonderful Ceroc dance with life. Ultimately, God retains control of the set structure of this world and his signs point to his desire for our lives. But he allows us the integrity and freedom to improvise within that structure and to choose the moves we make and the paths we take.

God is, therefore, not a coercive controller. He does not determine everything by unilaterally imposing his will. Instead, he participates in our lives, or as the book of Proverbs puts it: 'He shall direct your paths' (3:6; NKJV). So, he is constantly at work – inviting, cajoling, inspiring, nudging, pushing, suggesting and persuading. By doing so, he opens up the best possibilities in every situation. Sometimes he does this dramatically in profound spiritual experiences, like Moses at the burning bush or Saul on the road to Damascus. Most of the time, though, his call is quiet and persistent and his signs are revealed through seemingly non-consequential, ordinary events. As Bruce G. Epperly puts it: 'God seldom announces God's presence.'

Whether subtle or salient, God directs our paths and encourages us to recognise that he is standing alongside us. Squire Rushnell suggests the phrase 'GPS' for God's guidance in suggesting certain paths – 'God's Positioning System'. The concept of the 'self-made person' and the recent glorification of 'being yourself' are, therefore, problematic for Christians. Even Kierkegaard, the father of existentialism, a movement centred on determining our own development through our actions, held that we do not ultimately create ourselves. Rather, he suggested that we react, whether positively or negatively, to God's promptings and guidance. And so we may well grow and mature through events, relationships and circumstances, but God is interwoven through the thread of our lives, offering imaginative possibilities that champion love and flourishing.

## Meaning and order

In whatever form they may appear on our journeys, we are invited to open ourselves to recognising the goldfinches all around us. Like a child working out a dot-to-dot puzzle, we connect and interpret these signs in light of meaning. For us to be aware of God's fingerprints in our lives, we need to take steps to quieten the cacophony around us. When we face suffering or worldly pressures, it is easy to miss the voice that is subtly prodding and guiding. The centrality of prayer and medita-tion in our journeys cannot be understated. The theologian Richard Foster relates the discovering of God's signs in our lives to fostering a deep friendship with him. Like any meaningful friendship, it requires attentiveness, patience and a willingness to listen.

As I lay at home during my recovery, suffering and cut adrift from nor-mality, prayer was initially difficult. Slowly but surely, though, I began to open my heart to those meaningful moments of synchronicity, despite, and through, my pain. Played through my headphones, the Welsh hymn '*Arglwydd arwain trwy'r anialwch*' became an uplifting anthem in my dark moments. Sung in English as 'Guide me O thou great Redeemer', the direct translation from Welsh is 'Lord, lead me through the wilderness'. As we walk as 'pilgrims' through our 'barren land', Christians can recognise God's guidance and hear his voice. And so, in my pain and despair, questions surrounding whether God *sent* that goldfinch or whether he *prompted* me to look up the meaning of this small bird were less important than the fact that he *spoke* to me *through* this icon of healing and hope. The goldfinch became a sign of the kingdom in the midst of my despair, a source of hope at a time when I felt only hopelessness and a beacon of light when I was facing so much darkness.

In recognising such transcendent 'signs', we are challenging the prevalent worldview that we are insignificant beings in an arbitrary and aimless universe. By doing so, we are reassured that, despite the turbulence of our journeys, our lives are pregnant with meaning and order can be found in the chaos of our hurt. Recognising a caring, benevolent hand at work in our lives lifts us and gives us purpose and resilience. Research in Canada by psychologist Steve Hladkyj has shown that those who identify signs of meaning in everyday events score higher in their psychological health and are better adapted to stress. These people develop a stronger sense of well-being and inner strength resulting from viewing the world as orderly, friendly and responsive.

## Dangers in discernment

Still, great care needs to be taken in noticing and interpreting God's signs in our lives. We especially need to guard ourselves from imposing connections and patterns that do not exist between events and incidents, referred to as 'apophenia' by psychologists. At the heart of our journey needs to be intelligent, wise and reality-based discernment. After all, synchronicity is not magical thinking and we must not interpret incidences to confirm our own prejudices, wants or desires. Our discernment must include the recognition that not all random occurrences are profound. Sometimes, they may not even be so random or coincidental after all.

I was once contacted by a distressed parishioner who believed she was being targeted by dark, evil powers. I visited her with our diocesan deliverance officer to offer pastoral care and prayer. In our conversation with her, it soon became clear that her so-called spiritual attack was coming through Google and YouTube suggestions, which she believed were so coincidental that there had to be meaning in them. The reality is, of course, that online algorithms were far more likely to be behind the suggestions, rather than satanic powers. When we are suffering and distressed ourselves, we can often find ourselves making such distorted and false connections.

In fact, psychologists relate the human inclination to illusory pattern perception, when we falsely interpret meaning into every minute detail of our lives, to the huge increase in conspiracy theories in recent years. Coincidences in world-changing events and tragedies are often woven together with far-fetched conclusions. Terrorist atrocities, climate change, the European Union, pandemics, lockdowns, vaccinations and assassinations are falsely related to groups such as the 'illuminati', 'Zionists', 'communists' or a shadowy capitalist 'elite'. These are perceived to be working undercover in the secret corridors of power, carrying out nefarious plans. Christians especially need to guard themselves from such futile and reckless speculation. Researchers in the UK found that people who strongly define themselves as 'spiritual' are more susceptible to conspiracy theories, such as those around the Covid vaccine. Psychologists have dubbed this dangerous inclination as 'conspirituality'. In truth, sometimes there are no deeper meanings to random events and incidents. By embracing wild conspiracies not only do we ignore the complexity of God's world, but it can be dangerous and can detract from our life-giving engagement with God's presence. We cannot allow our belief in a personal God to lead us to interpret abnormal and distorted meanings into events, incidences and experiences.

Our call to discernment, then, requires self-awareness and clarity of thought. 'Dear friends,' writes John in his epistle, 'do not believe every spirit, but test the spirits to see whether they are from God, because many false prophets have gone out into the world' (1 John 4:1). Most importantly, signs need to be tested and judged by the only barometer that matters – God's love. Thus, we affirm those moments that relate to God's creative love, while weeding out those that might lead towards prejudice, destruction or hatred. As such, we come to identify God's voice as consistent with biblical witness and Christian tradition. 'Instinctively,' writes Richard Foster, 'we come to recognise the quality in the voice of God, for it is one of drawing and encouraging… it is full of grace and mercy.'

And the way of love, of course, is not always the easy journey or the most personally uplifting path. Wherever the sign might point, and however difficult the subsequent journey, it will always be in line with his loving purposes and will be consistent with his loving nature. Coincidence and synchronicity are gifts to us to ensure we walk faithfully on the path of love.

## Goldfinch moments

The 2019 film *The Goldfinch*, based on the novel by Donna Tartt, is centred on numerous coincidental events in the life of the central character, Theo. At the end of the film, his friend Boris sits with him in a bar, after having rescued him from a suicide attempt. He lists the synchronistic events, including Theo's unlikely survival of a terrorist attack as a child, that have finally led to a place of harmony and order and to the return of numerous stolen masterpieces, including Carel Fabritius' *The Goldfinch*. Boris concludes:

> Maybe good can come out of bad. If you hadn't, if I hadn't, maybe none of those paintings would be found. Maybe it's like a huge weather system rolling over and we just get blown, and maybe it's fate, or… why give a name? Just… life.

For Christians, moments such as my own goldfinch coincidence cannot simply be dismissed as mere fate or 'life'. After all, the signs we recognise in our lives relate to God's very being. They are rooted in his divine love, which is intimately involved with the world. They, therefore, either reassure us of his care and grace for us or inspire us to participate and cooperate in his boundless love through our own acts of justice and compassion. As such, our response shapes our journeys, bringing us nearer to, or further from, the kingdom of love, compassion and justice that God wills for his world. As Bruce G. Epperly puts it: 'God is always creative and God's creativity inspires our own creative attempts to bring goodness and beauty to the world.'

It is only when we actively commit to recognising God's Spirit in our synchronistic moments that we can take off our shoes and sit at the burning bush. As we notice more of these signs of the Spirit, Jung suggests we embark on a process of realising our spiritual potential and discovering our true identity. He terms this 'individuation' and suggests it leads us away from egocentrism and self-centredness and towards an inner wholeness. These signs therefore become 'kairos moments'.

The ancient Greeks used the word kairos to refer to a fixed or certain 'time', while chronos was a more chronological or linear reference to 'time'. Interestingly, they personified kairos as a god of luck and coincidence. In the New Testament, the use of kairos is significant, as it refers to God's chosen time, fixed by him and used for his purposes. And so our meaningful signs are kairos moments that are given as an opportunity for spiritual transformation and growth, as well as for compassion and connection with others.

As I recovered from my injury, I attuned myself to noticing these kairos signs. By doing so, I found strength in the idea, to use Hans Urs von Balthasar's terms, that I was now involved in a theodrama, where life had become about recognising God's loving kingdom breaking through, rather than in my own egodrama, where life is centred around my individual self. These signs became shafts of light in the darkness of my struggles. By opening ourselves to God's light in even the small and seemingly insignificant details of our everyday lives, a path of love can be illuminated and our journeys can be transformed. Recognising such signs can enrich our lives in ways beyond our understanding. They can reassure, comfort, inspire and challenge us. They can give us an inner peace. They can offer us hope.

# TIME TO REFLECT

- Think about the 'goldfinch moments' you have experienced in your own life, those times when God unexpectedly broke through the ordinary with synchronicity, clarity or grace.

- As you reflect on your journeys, how might you quieten the noise of daily life to notice more of these glimpses of God's kingdom shining through?

# 4

# Company

*One day, at long last, I stumbled from the dark woods of my own and my family's and my country's past, holding in my hands these truths. That love grows from forgiveness, that from destruction comes renovation, and that the evidence of God exists in our connections to one another. This much, at least, I've figured out. I know this much is true.*

Dominick Birdsey (played by Mark Ruffalo) in the 2020 TV series *I Know This Much Is True*

*Sharing pain is the most difficult thing, but it also turns out to be the only thing that makes life bearable.*

Kenneth Turan, film critic

## JOURNEY ONE: PILGRIM'S WAY

### Pilgrim companions

For many years I had a heroic, individualistic view of pilgrimage. When planning my North Wales pilgrimage, I pictured myself as a lone wanderer, like the walker from the famous painting of the German romantic Caspar David Friedrich, gazing down on the wonder of creation from a mountain summit. For the earliest Christian pilgrims, this image would have rung true, as travelling alone was believed to carry great spiritual merit. It did not take long, though, for practicality to prevail. Pilgrims soon realised that journeying with companions was far safer, especially when navigating treacherous paths beset by bandits. These days it is not so much the physical dangers of pilgrimage that can persuade us of the importance of fellowship, but rather the profound value of shared experiences and companionship along the way. In an old eastern proverb, a pupil asks: 'What is more important – the journey or the destination?' The teacher simply answers: 'The company.'

While there were plenty of sections of the Pilgrim's Way where I journeyed alone, the most unforgettable and heartwarming moments of the pilgrimage were the times spent in the company of others – friends and family who walked beside me, fellow travellers who became companions, and even strangers whose paths crossed mine along the way. The laughter, heart-to-heart chats, problems shared and in-depth discussions transformed the journey entirely. The most famous work of literature about pilgrimage, *The Canterbury Tales*, very much recognises the importance of companionship. Chaucer's masterpiece details a band of pilgrims being entertained and uplifted by each other's company and stories, as they travel together to the shrine of St Thomas Becket at Canterbury Cathedral. The importance of sharing the journey is referenced in the prologue to the work:

> *And wel I woot, as ye goon by the weye,*
> *Ye shapen yow to talen and to pleye;*
> *For trewely, confort ne myrthe is noon*
> *To ride by the weye doumb as a stoon.*

> *And I know well, as you go on your way,*
> *You will tell stories and play;*
> *For truly, comfort and joy is none*
> *If you're travelling as silent as a stone.*

The characters in Chaucer's epic have different backgrounds and social statuses. In the Middle Ages, people of diverse backgrounds would travel together, enjoying each other's company. Leaving lives and loves behind, they formed part of an entirely new entity – a band of pilgrims – forged and uplifted through talking and sharing. After all, without conversation, there would be no tales in *The Canterbury Tales*. Likewise in other journeys in literature, such as the very different 'pilgrimage' of Frodo and Sam in J.R.R. Tolkien's *The Lord of the Rings*, the principal blessing of often arduous journeys are the travellers simply enjoying each other's company – comforting, encouraging, laughing and singing.

## God revealed in people

The walking experience is certainly enhanced when someone walks alongside us. Social interaction changes both our experiences and ourselves in a fundamental way. Art critic Robert Hughes points out that a mouse behaves completely differently if a person walks into a room, just as a person's behaviour will change if they encounter a mouse. Not all of us would scream and jump on a chair, but we would certainly act differently if we noticed a small mammal in a room. If that is the case for a mouse, concludes Hughes, how much more do we change our behaviour, whether in subtle or significant ways, when we are in the presence of another human.

Not that having company on our travels is always a joy. The 15th-century pilgrim's diary *The Book of Margery Kempe* describes the challenges of journeying with others. Margery's peculiar habits, not least her tendency to pray out loud as she walked, began to grate on her fellow pilgrims. Frustration grew to the point where the group considered leaving her behind altogether. In the end, they struck a compromise – she could stay, but only if she sat at a separate table during meals! My own experience with companions on my pilgrimage could not have been more different. Most of my journey was spent alone, so I cherished the moments when family and friends joined me along the way, even those with their own quirks and idiosyncrasies! My solitary journey was transformed into something profoundly richer through their presence, and I was moved by their willingness to gift me their time and energy, especially as some travelled across the country to walk just one leg of the pilgrimage. God came to me revealed as friends, family and even strangers.

I deeply valued the unique gifts each person brought to the journey. Whether it was due to their compassion, generosity or simply their presence, these moments felt like true blessings. Kindness and connection make any journey so much richer. I remember one day when I was in excruciating pain with my knee. A friend who had travelled from Birmingham to walk with me for the day offered his shoulder each time I alighted from a ladder stile, which are so widespread in Eryri (Snowdonia). By the end of that day, my friend's shoulder was almost as sore as my knee!

At other times, my fellow pilgrims shared their wisdom and knowledge. My mother, for example, taught me to pay attention to the signs of spring at my feet. A keen amateur botanist, she would inform me of the names of the flowers that we passed, helping me appreciate them all the more. My sister, on the other hand, taught me some new skills when we heard the distressed bleating of a small lamb which had found itself stuck perilously on a road, separated from a field of her concerned relatives. Having inherited farming expertise from our *Taid* ('grandfather'), she taught me how to catch a lost sheep and we hoisted the frightened creature over the fence to the safety of her home.

## Heaven and mirth

The time with my sister also included so much laughter. Trekking across farmland, she insisted that I take a photograph to give to her husband, as she stood next to a sign which proclaimed *Rhybydd: Nid y cwn ond y wraig sy'n beryg* ('Warning: It is not the dogs who are dangerous, but the wife')! Charles Foster suggests that Christian pilgrimage differs from the spiritual journeys of other faiths in its emphasis on fun and laughter. This certainly rang true in my own experience, where humour often punctuated the struggles along the way. Surreal sights frequently left us pilgrims doubled over in laughter – a field of curious llamas, a roofless church, an abandoned car miles from the nearest road, a towering 20-foot plastic dinosaur in the middle of nowhere, and a garden crammed with life-sized, unnervingly realistic giraffes, aliens, cowboys and even models of Barack and Michelle Obama. On the Llŷn Peninsula, a painted stone on the cliffs urged us to 'walk faster and imagine banjos playing' and perfectly captured the absurd joy of the trail.

The laughter did not stop there. Conversations with fellow travellers, both old friends and new acquaintances, were just as entertaining. Lifelong friends brought cherished memories back to life, while new companions shared tales that were impossible not to enjoy – like the Methodist minister who had me in stitches recounting his escapades as a contestant on BBC's *Total Wipeout* and ITV's *Ninja Warrior*.

These moments of humour and connection added a rich, joyful layer to the pilgrimage and, in their midst, I felt as if we were treading on sacred ground. The religious concept of *hwyl* is something that is distinctive in Welsh history. The Welsh word *hwyl* is now in everyday usage to simply mean 'fun' or, when used as a departing remark, 'have fun'. Originally, though, it referred to a sense of uplifting joy in worship. The great Welsh revivals were, after all, rooted in religious fervour and joy. Wandering past old, long-closed chapels on my pilgrimage, as well as visiting those which were still open, I was conscious that the infectious and holy Welsh *hwyl* of the revivalists was still present in our pilgrim hearts as we walked.

## Angels in disguise

Even on those days when I walked alone, I connected with various people – hikers, church caretakers, museum curators, tourists, church wardens and even a few fellow pilgrims who were walking sections of the trail. The band of pilgrims in *The Canterbury Tales* were strangers before they met in the pilgrim's inn in Southwalk, with Chaucer noting they came into fellowship '*by aventure*' ('by accident'). I will not likely see or hear again from most of the people I encountered on my pilgrimage. Yet, with a few, I exchanged social media details, and we remain in touch to this day. Though our paths crossed only briefly, the bonds we formed in those moments continue to echo in our lives.

Yet, from childhood, we are taught to be wary of strangers. The phrase 'stranger danger' is drilled into us, and this is understandable, as our safety, especially as children, is paramount. But as we grow, this wariness often hardens into a tribal mindset, which can isolate us from those outside our familiar circles. This cautious approach stands in stark contrast to the Bible's perspective on strangers. Throughout the Old Testament, strangers are not merely tolerated, but are seen as a source of blessing. The Israelites are repeatedly instructed to welcome and care for the outsider, while strangers frequently become vessels of divine blessing – Jacob wrestling with the unknown man at Penuel, Abraham unknowingly welcoming angels into his home, Rahab sheltering Israelite spies, and the wealthy woman of Shunem offering hospitality to the prophet Elisha. The Bible paints a striking picture. The stranger is not someone to be feared, but someone through whom God is revealed.

Philosopher Will Buckingham writes of our deep, often overlooked, need for strangers. After losing his wife, he was not surprised to find comfort from the company of close friends. Far more unexpected was how much he found he needed strangers – people who knew nothing of his past, his grief or his story. These fleeting connections, he wrote, became 'a powerful antidote' to the paralysis of suffering. There is, after all, something liberating about engaging with those who are unentangled in our lives. Their presence can lift our burdens in unexpected ways. Sociologist Georg Simmel even suggested that strangers take on a priestly role, offering a modern-day confessional, simply by listening without judgement.

Yet, instead of embracing this, we are often driven by fear. The word *philoxenia*, meaning the love of the stranger, stands in direct opposition to xenophobia, the fear of strangers. The root of this term is in the New Testament, where Hebrews 13:2 urges believers: 'Do not forget to show hospitality to strangers [*philoxenia*], for by so doing some people have shown hospitality to angels without knowing it.' Of course, wisdom and safety matter. But pilgrimages offer moments where we can push beyond fear and hostility to embrace what philosopher Jacques Derrida called '*hosti-pet*' – *hosti* meaning stranger, *pet* meaning potential. Strangers are bearers of possibility and potential. Emmanuel Levinas went even further, suggesting that our relationship with a stranger is, in essence, a relationship with the future. And so I embraced strangers on my pilgrimage, not as an intrusion, but as an invitation. These angels in disguise were opportunities for me to glimpse something new, something divine and something yet to come.

Among these fleeting connections with strangers, one stands out – a remarkable moment of synchronicity during the final leg of my journey. As I reached Aberdaron and met up with my parents for the conclusion of the pilgrimage, I invited them to join me for the very last step – the boat trip to the sacred Ynys Enlli (Bardsey Island). My dad, however, needed some serious convincing. His paralysing fear of water made the idea of setting foot on a boat almost unthinkable. Reluctantly, he stepped on board, and as the boat pulled away from the shore, his anxiety was palpable. To distract himself, he struck up a conversation with the ferryman, mentioning that he used to visit the island on pilgrimages in the 1960s. During those trips, almost 60 years ago, he had formed a friendship with the ferryman. What followed was nothing short of extraordinary. The present ferryman revealed that he was the grandson of the man that my dad had befriended all those years ago. As the realisation sank in, my dad's fear of the water seemed to melt away, replaced by the joy of shared stories and connections spanning generations. The two talked animatedly on the way to the island and back again, bridging a gap of over half a century. My dad, who had once bonded with the ferryman in his youth, now found himself forging a friendship with his grandson – a beautiful, serendipitous ending to the pilgrimage.

Contrary to the image of the isolated pilgrim, human interaction on pilgrimages is central to the spiritual journeys that are taken. As we converse with those with whom we travel, we weave ourselves into their journey just as they become part of ours. It is a mutual exchange, a shared shaping of experience. When I read books, I often jot down notes in the margins – a habit that my younger self would have considered sacrilegious! When I revisit these scribbles, it reads as though I am having an intimate conversation with the author, responding to their thoughts across time. In much the same way, the conversations shared during a pilgrimage, whether with friends, family or strangers, leave their mark, not on pages, but on our hearts and minds. These exchanges, like inked impressions, become part of who we are, subtly shaping us, encouraging us and leaving behind a trace of the connection we shared. John O'Donohue suggests that our conversations reflect the Trinity, which he describes as an 'eternal interflow of friendship'. As we talk with each other, we experience a mutual habitation, a pouring out of one person into another and vice versa.

## The company of silence

As the days walking on my North Wales pilgrimage were long and physically exerting, much of the walking with friends and family was in silence. I was surprised by how powerful this was. When meeting our friends in coffee houses, we spend almost the whole time in conversation. Yet, when walking for up to ten hours a day, the 'space between the notes', to use Claude Debussy's phrase, becomes as important as the conversations. As St Ephraim of Syria is quoted as saying in *The Way of a Pilgrim*: 'Good speech is silver but silence is pure gold.'

When we go beyond words with our friends and family, we tread on sacred ground. Words have the power to enrich an experience, but they can also pull us away from the present moment. As the 1980s pop group Depeche Mode once sang, they can even do violence to silence. On my pilgrimage, I discovered the profound beauty of quietness. This was not the absence of sound, but a different kind of presence altogether.

After all, we rarely experience true silence. At home, silence is inter-rupted by the hum of a TV, the buzz of a phone or the distant roar of traffic. But on the pilgrimage, 'silence' became alive with the wonder of the natural world – birdsong drifting through the air, the rhythmic chirping of insects, the soft scurry of squirrels, the wind whispering through trees or the crash of waves against the rocks. This symphony of nature revealed that 'silence', far from being empty, is one of the richest sounds of all. In the TV series *Undone* (2019), Alma is given a hearing aid as a child. Later on, her father asks: 'Do you remember what you said about silence the first time you heard it?' Alma answers: 'I didn't know it sounded so alive.' The silence that modern pilgrims experi-ence is pregnant with beauty and meaning and is markedly different from our usual busy lives with their cacophony of man-made noises.

Jane Goodall describes reaching 'a new awareness that comes when words are abandoned'. She relates this to our early childhood, when all we can do is listen to the world as it goes by. Thus, silence has a way of drawing us back to a time when everything felt fresh, new and full of wonder. In their natural curiosity, children instinctively move beyond words and logic, fully embracing their intuition and immersing themselves in the present moment. By consciously reconnecting with our childlike nature and letting go of words, concepts and overthink-ing, we open ourselves to awe and wonder. In doing so, we step into the simplicity and beauty of God's kingdom. As Jesus taught: 'Truly I tell you, anyone who will not receive the kingdom of God like a little child will never enter it' (Mark 10:15).

Indeed, when I walked alone, without friends or family by my side, my company became this 'silence', as I welcomed a solitude that was so alien to my bustling city life. Norwegian explorer Erling Kagge once reflected that he felt 'much more lonely in large gatherings of people and in crowded towns than I did on my way to the South Pole'. His words resonate deeply, for there is a stark difference between loneliness and solitude. As anyone in pastoral work knows, loneliness can lead to unbearable despair. Yet solitude has always held a sacred place in the Christian tradition. It is a space where we can hear God's voice. In this sense, pilgrimage offers a unique gift to us – the chance to embrace that solitude and create room to encounter the divine. In his private journals, Kierkegaard describes a profound state where we transcend anger, jealousy, pride and self-pity. He calls this 'inwardness,' 'the God-relationship' or simply 'silence'. Pilgrimage invites us to enter this quiet, transformative space. And so, whether we are accompanied by the solitude of silence or the uplifting presence of people, our journeys have a way of opening the door to eternity.

## JOURNEY TWO: THROUGH INJURY AND DARKNESS

## Sacred friendship

During my long, difficult pilgrimage of recovery, family and friends were a constant source of hope and joy. Relationships provide us with inspiration and energy, but they are also restorative, bringing light to whatever darkness we are going through. In the barbarity of Auschwitz, Edith Eger described cooperation and companionship as the essential ingredients in getting through each day. They were, she writes, 'the name of the game'. Few of us will face such horrors as Eger endured, but, in my own pain and despair, friends and family certainly lifted my broken spirit.

In *The Pilgrim's Progress*, John Bunyan beautifully captures the dual role of friendship in times of suffering – it offers compassion and restores hope. Trapped in a dungeon by the oppressive Giant Despair, Christian spirals into depression. Yet, his companion Hopeful refuses to abandon him. Sitting by his side, he prays and encourages him, reigniting a spark of hope. Inspired, Christian recalls the key of promise hidden in his coat, which ultimately unlocks the dungeon door, setting them both free. That profound sense of liberation came to life for me as friends and family came to visit me on my red sofa, punctuating the overwhelming feeling of pain and despair with moments of comfort and encouragement.

Those who came to visit did not just share my burden – they helped transform it. As such, there is something deeply sacred about human companionship. It is a bond that reflects the covenant between God and Israel. When David turned to Jonathan for support in his time of need, he used the same Hebrew word that God employs to describe his steadfast love for his people: *hesed* – 'Show kindness [*hesed*] to your servant, for you have brought him into a covenant with you before the Lord' (1 Samuel 20:8). *Hesed* embodies God's faithful, loyal and enduring love (see Exodus 34:6), and in our moments of struggle, the kindness and compassion of friends can become a tangible reflection of that divine, covenantal love.

## Lifting each other in harmony

During my recovery, it was not always easy to see that the care and compassion so freely given were not just lifting my own spirits, but were also bringing purpose and meaning to those visiting me. More than anything, I was overwhelmed by the fear that I had become a burden, a parasite even, relying on the generosity of friends and family while giving little in return. Accustomed to being the caregiver in ministry, I now found myself in the vulnerable position of needing the very pastoral support I once provided. In a stark reversal of roles, I was visited regularly by kind parishioners and ordinands I was training. Years of ministry had ingrained in me the mistaken idea that pastoral care flowed in one direction. Allowing myself to lean into the support of others felt like swimming against the current of everything I had hitherto experienced.

Yet, as time went on, I began to see these visits differently. They were not signs of failure, but of grace. Gradually, I came to recognise their true value. Each encounter was humbling, each gesture of kindness uplifting and each moment of connection profoundly healing.

Most of the thought-provoking reflections shared by my school chaplain have faded from memory, but one has stayed with me for over 30 years. It was about reciprocity and the power of mutual support. He described a large choir singing in perfect harmony. As the audience listens, they never notice when a singer pauses to take a breath, because the others carry the melody seamlessly in their stead.

As I journeyed towards recovery, I found myself needing to stop singing. This was my time to take a breath, while my family and friends carried on the melody of life around me. They supported, visited, prayed, left gifts, and sent messages and cards. They did this instinctively and compassionately. And there may well come a day when they too will face hardship and might need to pause to take a breath. Others will then be there to sustain the melody for them. After all, we do not walk our journeys alone. As pilgrims, we travel alongside one another. As 16th-century poet John Donne put it: 'No man is an island, entire of itself; every man is a piece of the continent, a part of the main.' Together, we create the music of life, lifting each other in harmony when one voice needs to stop and rest.

## Shaped through relationship

Relationship is at the heart of what it means to be human. We do not exist in isolation. Rather, our very identity is shaped by the people around us, from our closest friends and family to the wider communities and nations we belong to. If, as St Augustine and Martin Luther suggest, sin is the act of turning inward on ourselves (*incurvatus in se*), then it blinds us to our deep need for others, deceiving us into believing we can thrive alone. No matter how independent or self-sufficient we like to think we are, connection remains essential to our well-being. As theologian Cynthia Bourgeault puts it: 'My true self is found only in communion with others.'

The philosopher Martin Heidegger suggests that we are fundamentally 'beings-with'. In other words, we are creatures shaped by our relationships and interactions with others. He challenged the individualistic ideas of thinkers like the fathers of modern political theory, John Locke and Thomas Hobbes, by maintaining that we are not isolated, self-contained beings. Instead, we are thrown into the world, deeply embedded in a shared social reality. Whether we are introverted or extroverted, whether we enjoy the company of others or not, our very identity is still formed through our connections and dealings with others. As Heidegger put it, a 'bare subject without a world' is an impossibility, as we can only truly exist within the context of our relationships.

Theologian Peter J. Leithart builds upon this concept by suggesting that our souls, like our bodies, do not have strict boundaries, but are 'porous and permeable'. In other words, our identities, personalities and characters are profoundly affected and formed through both the people we love and the strangers we meet. In this way, we take residence in each other. 'Others dwell in us, even as we pitch our tent in them', Leithart concludes.

It is through our interaction with other humans, then, that we become human ourselves. No wonder psychologists and sociologists are now emphasising the great benefits of friendship, both for society and for our individual well-being and health. In the documentary film *Garnet's Gold* (2014), the protagonist embarks on a journey to the remote Highlands, convinced he will uncover treasure hidden by Bonnie Prince Charlie centuries ago. Yet, despite his determination, the search yields nothing, and he returns home empty-handed. His frail, elderly mother, though, sees a deeper truth in his quest. For her, the real treasure lies not buried in the ground but in the friendships forged along the way. Gently, she reassures him:

> Gold isn't just stuff that you find in the ground or in a box marked 'X' on a map; you know, your life consists a lot of the time in thinking about the past and your place in it and the friends you had; and you gather up fragments of gold from those – gold dust!

# Neglecting friendship

The human need for connection and friendship crosses time, cultures and countries and hails from deep in our evolutionary past. Companionship and caring are ingrained in our genes, as Jane Goodall showed in her decades-long study of the relationships between the chimpanzees in the Gombe jungle in Tanzania. Not that fostering connection in our own lives is always straightforward. Our society has, after all, a rather mixed attitude to friendship. On the one hand, TV programmes and movies, such as the US comedy *Friends* and the franchises *Bad Boys*, *Sex and the City*, *Ice Age* and *Bill and Ted*, show the importance we place on close friendships. On the other hand, our world is highly transactional, and we are encouraged to work out what we can get out of things and people.

Little wonder that, over the past few decades, most of us have been living increasingly isolated lives. A recent British study found that one in ten of us do not consider ourselves to have close friends, while research in the US shows that this figure is a staggering one in four. In 2018, the UK government was so concerned with social isolation that a minister for loneliness was appointed, while in Japan 'rent-a-friend' companies are proving hugely popular and the trend is catching on elsewhere.

While I delighted in visits by kindly friends and appreciated the efforts of my family to sit and keep me company, I still felt a deep loneliness in the turmoil of my long journey of recovery. This reflected the fact that I had neglected so many of my friendships over the years. Although I had good and caring friends, I had become comfortably self-contained, and I rarely reached out to them or spent time with them. In a society obsessed with freedom, where we aim for sovereignty over our time and diaries, journalist Oliver Burkeman describes the one freedom which is always detrimental – the 'freedom not to see our friends'.

As I scrawled through endless social media posts while lying in pain on my sofa, it dawned on me that, while I was connected *to* so many, rarely was I connecting *with* anyone. In his book on the spiritual significance of friendship, theologian Drew Hunter offers a sobering perspective. When we reach the end of our lives and look back, he writes, we will not wish we had spent more hours at the office, binge-watching TV or scrolling endlessly through Instagram. What we might regret, however, is not investing more time in the friendships that truly give life its depth and meaning. He concludes: 'If you ask me what's best in life, I'm going to give you names.' Hunter's thesis is supported by Bonnie Ware, who reflected on her experience of nursing terminally ill patients. She observes that the principal regret of her patients is not having spent more time with their friends. 'Everyone misses their friends when they are dying', she concludes.

# ON OUR JOURNEYS

## Friendship and faith

For the Christian, at the heart of the gift and blessing of company lies the fact that our connection with others carries something of the divine. W.H. Auden captures this beautifully when he reflects on a conversation with a group of colleagues. Though they were not particularly close friends, he describes being 'invaded' by an irresistible 'power' simply through their presence. He wrote that his 'personal feelings towards them were unchanged – they were still colleagues, not intimate friends – but I felt their existence as themselves to be of infinite value and rejoiced in it'. For Christians, our relationships, whether intimate or fleeting, have something of this eternal quality.

After all, the communion within the Trinity is mirrored in our own relationships, if imperfectly. As we are made in the image of God (*imago Dei*), we reflect the nature of our creator. And so, just as the triune God exists in perfect relationship, we too are designed for connection. Relationships are not just something we do, but they are woven into the fabric of who we are. As theologian Timothy Keller puts it: 'The less you want friends, the less like God you are.'

We need to remember, though, that friendships come in many shapes and sizes, with no two exactly alike. Some of us thrive in the buzz of social gatherings, while others prefer the quiet of one-to-one conversations. Some friendships flourish online, while others deepen through shared experiences in person. We each navigate relationships in ways that reflect our personalities, needs and preferences. Stanley Hauerwas highlights the profound role of friendship in the lives of those with complex disabilities. In his study of L'Arche communities around the world, he demonstrates how deep, meaningful friendships can grow between those with and those without intellectual disabilities. But for this to happen more widely, he argues, we must let go of rigid ideas about what friendship should look like. This challenge extends into all our lives.

Recent research has also shown that many neurodivergent people approach friendship differently. Ann Memmott, an autism expert who has advised both the Church of England and the UK Parliament, suggests that Jesus himself had autistic friends. Nicodemus in John's gospel, for example, displayed so many hallmarks of neurodivergence – he took things literally, sought quiet spaces over crowds and relied on rules to navigate the world. Yet Jesus never demanded that he change this. Instead, he simply welcomed him as he was, affirming his friendship without condition. When we cling too tightly to narrow definitions of friendship, we risk overlooking the divine image in those who relate differently. The *imago Dei* is not reserved for those who fit a particular social mould – it is present in every person and in every kind of relationship. God is found in the full spectrum of human friendships.

So, friendships are holy in the sense they reflect God's character. The concept of God as a God of friendship goes beyond the traditional, hierarchic images of the divine (e.g. father/children, shepherd/lambs). The theologian Jürgen Moltmann emphasises the importance of 'openness' as we root our friendships in God's character. Closed friendships seek to preserve the individual, and, like closed societies and closed churches, they are insular and self-absorbed. The gospel, though, calls us beyond our comfort zones, inviting us to embrace friendships built on trust and vulnerability. True friendship has the power to dismantle hierarchy, creating relationships of openness rather than control. As Jesus told his disciples at the last supper: 'I no longer call you servants… Instead, I have called you friends' (John 15:15). In a world marked by deepening social, political and ecclesial mistrust, this vision of friendship upends the status quo, offering a way of connection that is rooted, not in status or power, but in love.

## Greater love has no one

My mother tongue can help nourish this understanding of the divine notion of friendship. The Welsh language distinguishes between two forms of 'knowing'. First, we have *gwybod*, which is the knowing of things. Second, there is *adnabod*, which is knowing a person.

This second word, *adnabod*, is a complex and rich word. Welsh poet Waldo Williams suggests that relationships that offer us meaning are related to *adnabod* and they are only possible when God's own personhood is present. Luke's gospel describes the disciples on the road to Emmaus as 'knowing' (*epiginóskó*) their master when they finally recognise the risen Jesus. The Welsh translators of the Bible translated that Greek word as *adnabod*. So, God is quite literally present in the friendship on the dusty road to Emmaus. Another Welsh poet, Mererid Hopwood, observes that *adnabod* embodies love in 'a fraternal, unified way', intertwining friendship and family. She beautifully describes *adnabod* as 'the gift that ties us together as a family.'

Building on this, theologian Dorian Llywelyn introduces another Welsh word, *perthyn*, to expand this idea. *Perthyn* carries a dual meaning – to 'belong' and to be 'related'. And so, in a Christian context, both *adnabod* and *perthyn* point to a heavenly vision of universal brotherhood. They allow friendship to become a reminder that we are all interconnected as a family of loving brothers and sisters in Christ.

The scriptural witness further relates friendship to love. Of the six Greek words for love, only *agape* and *philia* are used in the New Testament. *Agape*, the universal, sacrificial love of God, has been a central focus of Christian theology for centuries. In contrast, *philia* has often been overlooked. In the ancient world, *philia* was seen as an exclusive and limited form of love, reserved for close friends. For Christians, this might seem to place it beneath *agape*, which is unconditional, unlimited and inclusive. This traditional emphasis on *agape*, championed over and above *philia*, has even led some to suggest that Jesus might have been, in the words of Joseph Epstein, 'maybe, at least obliquely, anti-friendship'.

Yet, while the ancient world often distinguished between 'friendship love' (*philia*) and 'unconditional love' (*agape*), the New Testament blurs these lines. In scripture, *agape* and *philia* are used interchangeably, with both used to describe the love of God *and* the love between friends. In fact, John's gospel directly connects *agape* to friendship, suggesting that these two forms of love are not as separate as they might seem – 'Greater love [*agape*] has no one than this: to lay down one's life for one's friends' (John 15:13). So, whether the New Testament speaks of *agape* or *philia*, it is clear that, for Jesus, friendship lies at the heart of his mission and it is deeply intertwined with God's unconditional and boundless love.

This is echoed in the entire history of redemption, from Genesis to Revelation, which Timothy Keller refers to as 'a giant, cosmic act of friendship'. In the opening chapters of the Bible, Adam's isolation marks an incomplete aspect of creation (Genesis 2:18). This highlights that life without friendship is fundamentally lacking. We are not meant to live alone, as it is only through relationships that we can truly reflect the relational love at the very heart of God's being. It is no wonder that biblical writers envision a future rooted in mutual harmony. In scripture, hope is never an individual pursuit but a shared, communal reality. Early Christian thinkers like Irenaeus describe creation's destiny as 'divinisation', a profound union with one another in God, in which all of creation is brought into perfect harmony. Drew Hunter therefore suggests that our friendships today are 'an experience of inaugurated eschatology'. In other words, our relationships allow the future joy of God's kingdom and the new creation to break into the present. In the bonds we share, not least within the church, a community of Jesus' friends, we catch a glimpse of the glorious age to come. As Hunter concludes: 'History ends with neither a bang nor a whimper, but with the laughter of friends.'

The centrality of friendship in the redemption narrative is seen most vividly on the cross. After all, it is against the profound backdrop of Golgotha that Jesus speaks about the power of friendship (John 15). The cross, Jesus' ultimate act of self-giving love, is not only the corner-stone of our faith but also the greatest expression of true friendship. 'It is in this thoroughly human love of Jesus for his friends', writes biblical scholar Richard Bauckham, 'that the divine love for the world takes human form.' When we become his disciples, we are invited into this friendship, a gift we are called to receive and then extend to others.

Celtic spirituality develops this in the concept of soul friendship (*anam cara*), which recognises that Jesus himself is present in our relation-ships. In this sense, Irish poet John O'Donohue maintains that our friendships are sacramental. Through them, we tread on divine ground and are granted intimate access to the mystery of God. The company we keep can transform and transfigure us and forge our friendships into, in O'Donohue's words, an 'extensive and intensive force'.

## Encountering Jesus in the other

Actor Michael J. Fox was diagnosed, aged 29, with young-onset Par-kinson's disease. Over 20 years later, he wrote powerfully about how he undertook brutal and challenging physiotherapy following major surgery on a growth on his spine. He acknowledges how, in some ways, it was a journey he had to tread alone as his rehabilitation was rooted in inner strength and independent dedication. 'This is an inside job,' he writes, 'it only works if I believe.' However, he also recognises that, without the love and support of friends, family and health workers, his recovery would have been insurmountable.

Similarly, all our journeys will have moments that we must face alone. There are solitary pathways where we walk with only God's Spirit for strength. Yet, our travels are also shaped, inspired and enriched by the people who walk alongside us – friends, family, colleagues and even strangers. This was true of my pilgrimage across North Wales. But it was equally true in the season of recovery that followed. That recovery was an inward journey, one I had to navigate with God's guidance, step by determined step. But through the heartache and tears, the love and support of family and friends became my lifeline. In those many months, I felt Jesus' presence powerfully, through every act of kindness, every word of encouragement and every gesture of care from those around me.

Theologian Dietrich Bonhoeffer powerfully reflected on encountering Jesus in the other. In the face of the turmoil, suffering and oppression of Nazi Germany, this conviction became central to his theology and the foundation for his life of friendship and community. Bonhoeffer challenges us to move beyond viewing God as a distant, invisible deity. Instead, he urges us to recognise God in the flesh and bones of those around us, in our friends and neighbours who, like us, carry the full weight of human experiences and emotions. Through them, God stands with us, for us and beside us. When we are shown love by others, they step into our story, share our pain and embrace our journey. Thus, in a world dominated by transactions and exchanges, company offers a striking contrast. At its heart is grace, a gift freely given and received, transforming both the giver and the receiver in profound ways. 'We are a part of everyone we have loved,' concludes James Bryan Smith, 'and they are a part of us.'

# TIME TO REFLECT

- How important is the presence of others in the journeys you are walking right now?

- Think of the times when friends, neighbours, colleagues or even strangers have walked beside you. How have you experienced God's love and peace through their presence and support along the way?

# 5

# Dependence

*God gives and loves by nature as surely as a duck quacks by nature.*
Rowan Williams, theologian

*If the only prayer you said in your life was 'Thank You' that would suffice.*
Meister Eckhart, mystic

## JOURNEY ONE: PILGRIM'S WAY

## The vulnerability of trust

Charles Foster has claimed that 'every pilgrimage is a journey backwards; every pilgrim's step is a step toward his childhood'. In light of my teenage years, when I would look out longingly at Ynys Enlli after a tiring day surfing at Hell's Mouth, my pilgrimage was quite literally a step back in time for me. But it also recalled my childhood in another unexpected way. During my walk, I discovered more about dependence and trust than I had in the previous decades of my life.

As children, we are entirely reliant on others, and it is through that dependence that we first grasp how essential trust is to our growth and well-being. I vividly remember watching my son learn to walk. He had to learn to trust both his own little legs and his family who were supporting him. As he grew tired of the demands of crawling, he started to stand up and gingerly take a few steps before taking a tumble. Each time we would pick him up, comfort him and watch him start the process again. His many falls, cushioned by his nappy, did not dampen his determination. On my journey along the Pilgrim's Way, I quickly learnt that I had to embrace the possibility of falling, both metaphorically and literally, and trust that God would pick me up and guide me forward.

Control and trust are, of course, closely related, not least because of our tendency to trust those things that we believe we can control. We are wired to try to control everything and everyone, from our health to our work colleagues. We go through life striving to secure the outcomes we desire, as if grasping at control can guarantee certainty. On pilgrimages, though, we quickly learn that we can control little. The weather, our sustenance, the condition of the footpaths, and our aching and tired bodies are largely beyond our control. And so on pilgrimage we become vulnerable, as we put our trust in something greater that is guiding, nourishing and sustaining us. In a world where trust is constantly tested, whether through manipulative advertising or deceptive politics, it is little wonder we often feel the need to keep our guard up. But, on pilgrimage, we lean on others and trust in the care of a greater, unifying power, and so our vulnerability transforms from a perceived weakness into a profound strength.

## From independence to interdependence

In recent years, the whole idea of dependence has been denigrated, often viewed as a weakness to avoid at all costs. As individuals and as a society, none of us wishes to become dependent on others, whether through disability, illness or life circumstances. Independence, by contrast, is celebrated as the ultimate goal. We raise our children to become self-reliant adults, capable of managing their lives without our intervention. Later in life, many of us cling to our independence with stubbornness and pride, resisting any notion that we might need help to truly flourish.

Independence certainly has its place and can be important for thinking and acting effectively. But it is actually interdependence that lies
at the heart of a well-rounded life and a thriving society. We depend
on countless others for so much, whether it is the farmers and workers who stock our supermarkets or the healthcare professionals who
care for us in times of need. Beyond that, we are also deeply reliant on
creation itself – on trees for the air we breathe, insects to maintain the
delicate balance of ecosystems, and plants and animals for nourishment. Pilgrimages bring this reality into sharp focus, grounding us in
the daily awareness of how deeply interconnected we are, not just with
other people, but with the natural world that sustains and shapes us.

Reminders of this dependence were scattered along my walk on the
Pilgrim's Way. As in my childhood, my parents were there for me every
step of the way – providing food, moral support and even a place to
stay, as both their home and their holiday home were on the pilgrim
path. Likewise, I found myself sustained by the encouragement and
support of others. Some sent supportive texts or emails, while others
provided in my moments of need, filling my water bottles up in their
houses or, having read about my walk on my blog, leaving tea and
biscuits for me in their churches.

There were, though, also other moments of provision and support
that spoke to me of a greater, synchronistic connection. On the second
day of my journey, I made a basic error by underestimating how much
water I would need on a sunny, spring day. After trekking over ten
miles, with five still ahead to complete, I drained the last drops from
my water bottles. An overwhelming thirst began to take hold, the kind
that made every step feel heavy. Checking my map, I saw that the small
hamlet of Tremeirchion was just ahead. This was my last chance for
relief, as there would be no other village before I reached that night's
destination. Tremeirchion did not have a shop, but I spotted a sign
for the Salusbury Arms, a pub named after a local noble family that
are even mentioned in a poem by Shakespeare. My hope of a drink
there quickly faded as I arrived to find a note on the door on the pub
informing me it was closed for the rest of the week. With my mouth

parched and my heart sinking, I stumbled into the quiet sanctuary of Corpus Christi Church, hoping against hope. I soon found that there were no taps or running water there. Desperate, I wandered into the sacristy, and there was my holy grail – a single unopened bottle of water on a table. I left a few coins and scribbled a note of explanation and thanks to the vicar. That small bottle of water quenched my thirst and gave me the strength to finish the day's journey. The experience was a humbling reminder of how fragile life can be and how deeply we depend on others.

## Food, glorious food

In fact, my awareness of my basic needs was transformed during my journey. Early into the walk, I noticed something extraordinary – food and drink began to taste completely different. Exhaustion and exhilaration transformed even the simplest fare into a feast. Perched on logs or boulders, gazing out at breathtaking views, I found unexpected delight in a humble diet of raisins and water. The warmth of the raisins in my stomach and the surge of energy they provided became daily sources of gratitude and joy. What had once seemed ordinary now felt like delicious nourishment for both body and soul. In reflecting on his arduous 58-day ski to the North Pole, Erling Kagge describes how, as each gruelling day passed, his food began to be more appetising and its taste more flavoursome. In the days before reaching his destination, he describes his food as tasting simply 'heavenly'.

In our fast-paced, abundant society, we often lose sight of the true value of food and drink. We grab snacks on the go, rush through meals without a second thought, or worse still, eat mindlessly in front of the TV or while scrolling on our phones. But on pilgrimage, a remarkable shift happens. There is a profound freedom in savouring just what we need, rather than mindlessly consuming as much as we want. Each bite becomes an intentional act, a moment to truly appreciate the nourishment it provides.

In a conversation between Winnie the Pooh and Piglet, they discuss their first thought each morning. The little bear says that he wakes and thinks: 'What's for breakfast?' Piglet says his first thought is: 'I wonder what's going to happen exciting today?' After a moment of thought, Pooh asks: 'Isn't that the same thing?' On a pilgrimage, we are primed for enjoying food with the radical amazement and wonder of Pooh's words. As we refuel our tired bodies and minds, the texture and taste of even basic food satisfies us in ways that excessive eating can never do.

The Greek philosopher Epicurus wrote to a friend that 'bread and water confer the highest possible pleasure when they are brought to hungry lips'. Epicurus was the first to observe that true satisfaction comes when we avoid overindulgence. Later, Christian contemplatives and monastics echoed this wisdom, teaching that excess not only dulls our joy but also distances us from the divine. Instead, it is in savouring life's simplest essentials that we draw closer to God's presence. As Meister Eckhart put it: 'You do not find God by adding anything to your soul, you find him by taking things away.'

## An attitude of gratitude

Each time I ate on pilgrimage, I would pray a prayer of thanks for sustenance, surroundings and safety. Slowly but surely, gratitude became a constant companion on my walk. Almost all languages have a word for 'gratitude'. Yet a perfect storm of technology, consumerism and materialism has occurred in recent years that has inclined us towards ingratitude. As Rupert Sheldrake writes:

> If the universe is nothing but an unconscious mechanical system governed by eternally fixed laws of nature, and if evolution occurs through the blind forces of chance and necessity, and if the universe is entirely purposeless, and if biological evolution has no ultimate meaning, then what can we be grateful for or to?

And so our society often nurtures entitlement rather than gratitude. The act of paying for something can subtly make us feel as though we deserve it, simply because we have exchanged money. Technology takes this even further, depersonalising our interactions and widening the gap between us and a thankful heart. Pausing at a self-checkout machine in a supermarket to express heartfelt gratitude would likely earn us more than a few puzzled looks from fellow shoppers!

One of the real blessings of pilgrimage is that it that can help build a meaningful connection through the deep sense of gratitude it fosters. There is something in gratitude that acknowledges we are all interconnected and interdependent. Down the years, so many people, whether friends, family, acquaintances or strangers, have helped us grow and flourish in all sorts of ways. Similarly, we ourselves support and help others in ways that are beyond our knowledge or comprehension. There is a flow in gratitude – a flow of giving and receiving. This flow is essential to individual and societal well-being. No wonder all the major world religions relate gratitude to dependence. When we acknowledge our reliance, not just on others, but on the countless living organisms that sustain our ecosystem and our very survival, we are naturally drawn to a deep gratitude to the ultimate source of life. Walking the Pilgrim's Way, tracing the steps of countless pilgrims through the centuries, I felt that innate attitude of gratitude more powerfully than ever before.

# JOURNEY TWO: THROUGH INJURY AND DARKNESS

## Relinquishing control

In my very early days of languishing on the red sofa during my second journey, feeling forlorn and in pain, I could not have felt more detached from those pilgrimage moments of dependence on, and gratitude to, a

higher power. When our lives fall apart, searching for God in the fragments of debris can be a thankless task. It is even more challenging
to place our trust in that God who feels hidden from view. The day
before I made the crossing to Ynys Enlli, when I had visited Aberdaron,
I remember seeing one particular stone in the large pile of pilgrim stones
outside the museum. Pilgrims had been invited to write anything that
their journeys had put on their heart, and each stone was adorned with
colourful writing. Before I wrote my own word on a stone, I glanced
down at the array of words. A large circular stone with a single Welsh
word written in orange chalk stood out – *ymddiriedwn* ('trust').

Many of us struggle to relinquish control of events and situations.
My own tendency is to resort to catastrophising and ruminating on
worst-case scenarios. When my son was seven years old, I remember
leaving him in a football camp for the day. We said our goodbyes and,
as I was walked away, I looked back to see him standing alone, with
the other children playing around him. But this was no stereotype of
an inconsolable child crying as his parents leave him in school. The
tears, instead, were coming from his dad's eyes. Other parents seemed
far more sanguine about leaving their children. My mind, though, was
envisaging my precious son isolated and lonely all day. The worry bled
into my work, and I had to stop myself from driving back to the sports
centre to save my son from the anguish and pain I imagined him facing.
When I picked him up at the end of the day, though, he greeted me
with a beaming smile, bursting with excitement as he shared stories
of a great day of football and all the new friends he had made. Allowing things simply to unfold and trusting that things will work out is a
challenge for so many of us.

## Our changeable lives

Like the changeable sea, our lives are in constant motion. Embracing
this truth can help us anchor ourselves in trust, even when the storms
of struggle make it feel elusive. There will be times when all seems
tranquil and we are blessed with joy, pleasure and celebration. But

sometimes storms rage around us and we face pain, anxiety or grief. A few months on from my Pilgrim's Way walk, as I lay in pain on my sofa, I was visited by a kindly parishioner who rather cryptically suggested: 'You need to face your pain like the Great Bear Hunt.' It was only when my youngest chose *We're Going on a Bear Hunt* as his bedtime story a few nights later that I understood something of what she meant. In this classic children's book, we join a family as they search for a bear by facing various challenging terrains – forest, mud, long grass and snow. With each different environment, we are told that 'We can't go over it; We can't go under it; Oh no, we have to go through it!'

Sometimes our times of pain, hurt or affliction are unavoidable. As Jesus told his disciples, sometimes there is no other path other than to take up your cross (Luke 9:23). At those times, we have to 'gird up our loins' (Job 40:7, RSV) and face our misery head on. We cannot be like rugby players, skilfully sidestepping opponents. Instead, we are forced by our circumstances to be like American football players, confronting opposite numbers head-on by crashing into them. For Christians, though, this is not a passive acceptance of our fate. Rather, we trust that we can depend on God during the darkest of moments. Such a trust demands surrendering our need to control events or people. We give ourselves over to something bigger and more glorious. By doing so, to again use theologian Hans Urs von Balthasar's terms, we discard our egodrama and embrace the theodrama.

Learning to trust helped transform my anxious thoughts. It seemed ironic that this newfound trust was not predicated on any recovery that I hoped would happen in the future. Rather, it was grounded in the grit and grind of my everyday struggle. It was trusting that God was present in the process rather than the outcome – that he was walking alongside me on the journey, not waiting at the destination. I began to notice and cherish those daily glimpses of God's joy and grace piercing through the pain and frustration, like rays of hope in the dark. This was as powerful a healing as any physical cure could offer. As an old proverb puts it: 'Sometimes God calms the storm, but sometimes God calms the sailor.'

# Receiving the kingdom like a child

This second pilgrimage, though, was also a raw and visceral reminder of my utter dependence on other people in my life. Trust and dependence are woven into the fabric of life from the very beginning. The moment we latch on to our mother's breast, we instinctively trust that nourishment will come and life-giving milk will flow. Human offspring are unusual in having a longer developmental period after birth, which allows for more complex brain development and social learning. This leaves children dependent on adults for many years, whether for feeding, safety, shelter, care and support.

Yet as we enter adulthood, our dependence on others does not wane. In every detail of our lives, we remain fundamentally reliant on others – for our food, clothing, medical care, housing, utilities and so on. This is already an everyday reality, but illness and disability exacerbate our dependence. As I walked through the desolate landscape of pain, it quickly became clear that even my simplest tasks felt beyond my grasp, leaving me unable to rely on my own strength. My wife, Sandra, and even my young children, were assisting me with basic tasks, such as putting on my socks or tying my shoelaces. The impact this situation was having on them was hard for me to understand and accept. On one occasion, as I awoke from a daytime sleep on my red sofa, I felt a little hand reaching up inside the back of my T-shirt and heard the whispered voice of my four-year-old son: 'Lord Jesus, please make daddy's back get better'.

An East African tribe, the Kikuyu, have a custom of putting newborns in a basket outside their house so that the elders can walk past and give them a blessing. The blessing is not imparted with words. Rather, each adult in the community walks by and spits on the infant. This may seem somewhat shocking, but it is done as a recognition that, from birth, the whole village will be involved in raising the child. The dependence on others will continue into adulthood, as we not only assist others in their need and also embrace the assistance of others.

Jane Goodall recounts a story about the birds of the sky arguing as to who could fly the highest. The resplendent eagle was confident he would win. He flew slowly and steadily, higher and higher, passing all his feathered friends. Eventually, he could fly no higher and felt delight at victory. At that moment, a tiny wren hidden on his back, nestled in his fine feathers, took the opportunity to spread her wings and fly a little bit higher, thus snatching the crown from the eagle. All of us, writes Goodall, are like that little wren. Everything we are, everything we achieve, every freedom we have and every skill we possess, we owe to others, whether through their teaching, kindness or sacrifice.

The eagle has long been a symbol of spiritual power and strength. In the Old Testament, the eagle represents God's loving care of his people, pictured as carrying its young on its wings (Exodus 19:4; Deuteronomy 32:11). Goodall's story can, therefore, be understood as being about more than dependence on our fellow humans. It is a powerful and encouraging image of security and of our dependence and trust in God. Each of us is carried and sustained by God's power. Never is this truer than when we are facing adversity and suffering. He provides energy when we are exhausted, strength when we are sinking and hope when we are helpless.

## Life as a gift

Despite the pain and anguish of my second pilgrimage, I began to recognise life as a precious gift. From the moment God breathed into Adam's nostrils (Genesis 2:7), everything about our existence has been a gift to us. In fact, 'giving' can be seen as central to God's trinitarian character. Some theologians picture the Trinity as eternally giving-and-receiving love, with the Father giving to the Son, the Son receiving and the Holy Spirit returning to the Father. Miroslav Volf presents a more communal and harmonious pattern – with all three divine persons giving, receiving and returning eternally: 'One does not give first, with the result that the others would be indebted, but all give in the eternally moving circle of exchanges.' Thus, giving lies at the very heart of God's nature, with each person of the Trinity endlessly pouring love into the other.

This eternal cycle of giving forms the foundation of our own relationship with God. At the heart of this is God's unmerited and unconditional gift of love. After all, the word 'grace' is the translation of one of the Greek words for 'gift' (*charis*). 'In love he predestined us for adoption to sonship through Jesus Christ, in accordance with his pleasure and will – to the praise of his glorious grace, which he has freely given us in the One he loves', writes the apostle Paul (Ephesians 1:4–6). Karl Marx saw the concept of freely given grace as a key reason to reject Christianity, perceiving it as demeaning and stifling. To him, the idea of relying on God undermined human independence: 'A man who lives by the grace of another considers himself a dependent being.' For Marx, true human freedom required breaking free from dependence and thus learning to stand on our own.

There is, though, nothing belittling or constraining about God's grace. It is as liberating as it is radical. Grace goes beyond the transactional way of viewing the world which has defined our lives for many centuries and it bucks the contemporary trend to idealise independence. Affluent societies do not tend to grasp the wonder of a freely bestowed grace. Wanting for very little, we define ourselves by our earnings and we value independent, self-made success. Yet, the real wonder of God's gifts is that we can do nothing to warrant or win them. The reformer Martin Luther pictured God's gifts flowing down to us in one direction, like water running down the mountainside. 'The love of God flows forth and bestows good', he wrote. God does not give to receive glory, praise or thanks. There is no 'holy self-seeking' in him, as Karl Barth puts it. Instead, he gives freely and abundantly because it is fundamental to his character.

For Christians, responding to God's gifts begins with a vital first step – receiving his grace. This is not done with pride or self-reliance but with a posture of expectant and joyful humility. Having an incapacitated and despondent dad during such a formative time in his life could not have been easy for my four-year-old son. Wanting to show my gratitude for his patience and support, I decided to surprise him with a gift. I sat him on his bed and asked him to hold out his hands for a special surprise. Just as I was about to place a few packs of his beloved football cards in his tiny hands, my phone buzzed – it was my bishop calling. I stepped out to take the call, expecting to be gone for just a moment, but it stretched into ten minutes. When I finally returned to my son's room, I was met with a sight that stopped me in my tracks. There he sat, exactly where I had left him, with his eyes closed, arms outstretched and hands open. He was waiting patiently, his face glowing with excitement and expectation. This posture of expectant, humble receptivity spoke to me of how Christians need to be as receivers of God's gifts. The words 'we are beggars, that is true' were scribbled on a slip of paper that was found in reformer Martin Luther's pocket when he died. It is, however, not through passive pleading that we should receive God's gifts. Rather, we need to be bright-eyed and expectant for the blessings he showers on us.

Miroslav Volf, however, warns us not to see God as 'our heavenly Santa Claus'. He does not gift us his blessings simply to make us feel good, fulfil our desires or solve our problems. God's giving makes demands on us too. This is the second step in our response to God's grace – first we receive, and then we pay it forward. God may not expect anything in return, but, by the very nature of grace, we cannot help but be inspired by his gift. 'The true God gives so we can become joyful givers', writes Volf, 'and not just self-absorbed receivers.'

The Reformation's focus on 'justification by faith alone' has often made us cautious about emphasising the importance of our actions. Yet, loving actions naturally flow from genuine faith – they are its living, breathing evidence. Christians are not like children who hoard sweets in their pockets and refuse to share. Instead, our natural response to God's freely given grace is to glorify the giver by living out those two great commandments – love of God and love for others. In other words, the bountiful gifts of God inspire us to compassion, kindness and generosity in our own lives.

# ON OUR JOURNEYS

## Paying it forward

The call of the Christian in all our journeys is to reflect the eternal, trinitarian process of giving and receiving. God gives to us to help us flourish. In turn, we become a 'living sacrifice' (Romans 12:1) as we give ourselves to others to support and nurture their flourishing. In C.S. Lewis' *The Lion, the Witch, and the Wardrobe*, each child receives a special gift from Father Christmas when he returns to Narnia after years of absence. But it becomes clear that these gifts are not just for the children themselves. Instead, they serve a greater purpose, becoming blessings for others as channels of God's grace. Susan's horn becomes Lucy's salvation when she is attacked by a wolf. Peter's sword and shield empower him to bring freedom and peace to Narnia. Lucy's cordial, with its healing properties, saves many lives, including that of her brother Edmund, who hovers on the brink of death.

In the same way, we are called to be channels for the gifts God gives us. This applies not only to the gift of his grace, which inspires us to love others, but also to the unique, personal gifts with which he blesses us. Whether material possessions, intangible qualities like creativity and wisdom, or talents such as artistic or athletic abilities, these gifts can flow through us to bless others. 'Freely you have received; freely give', Jesus told his disciples (Matthew 10:8).

The idea of 'paying forward' gifts may feel unfamiliar to those of us in the west, where receiving a gift often means gratefully keeping it. Yet, in many cultures, the ethics of gift exchange is strikingly different and is rooted in the expectation that gifts are shared and their blessings multiplied. Cultural critic Lewis Hyde delves into the Native American tradition of paying gifts forward. In this practice, gifts are not meant to be hoarded. Instead, to ensure the cycle of generosity continues, a gift is either given away or replaces something of similar value that is given to someone else. Hyde compares this to 'the way a billiard ball may stop when it sends another scurrying across the felt, its momentum transferred'. In other words, gifts keep going and going, bringing joy to many people.

Similar traditions are to be found in other cultures, with folk tales from the Uduk tribe in north-east Africa to the Celts in the Scottish Highlands teaching that those who do not pay gifts forward will be punished. Giving is, therefore, to be viewed as a constantly flowing river, and the challenge is for us to become channels for its current. 'When someone tries to dam up the river,' writes Hyde, 'one of two things will happen: either it will stagnate or it will fill the person up until he bursts.'

So, we ourselves should not be the final destination of God's gifts. God gives so we continue the giving by living out his love and peace in our daily lives. Even the most vulnerable and broken people can become imitators of Christ (Ephesians 5:1) and his love is made manifest in their lives. Good things flow into us from God and, as Martin Luther put it, 'these good things flow from us on to those who have need of them'. And he might have added that the flow continues as others 'pay it forward' through their own compassion and care for others.

## Gratitude breaking through hardship

Yet, there is also another step in our response to the gifts God bestows on us – gratitude. Anthropologist Marcel Mauss describes gratitude as a natural 'counter-gift', something we feel compelled to give in return. Expanding on this idea, Elizabeth Oldfield suggests that Martin Luther's emphasis on the freely given nature of grace might have caused us to overlook an important truth – that even grace involves a kind of reciprocity. Not that God's gifts to us are about a transactional exchange. They do, though, inspire a response of gratitude – a deep, heartfelt acknowledgment of the love we have received. This is, in Oldfield's words, 'an incredibly powerful spiritual technology – an antidote to hedonic adaptation'.

Such a gratitude lies at the very heart of our reliance on God, even in the midst of pain and hardship. Kierkegaard came to understand the profound significance of gratitude in the Christian life through a deeply traumatic experience that reshaped his faith and perspective. In 1841, he broke off his engagement with his fiancée- Regine Olsen and was deeply haunted by her final words as he walked away: 'So, after all, you have played a terrible game with me.' Later in life he came to realise that Regine had been a precious gift from God, which he had failed to truly appreciate. This revelation transformed him, and he dedicated the rest of his life to embracing God's gifts with gratitude and humility. To remind himself of this profound commitment, and despite Regine marrying another man, he had her engagement ring recast as a diamond cross which he wore until his dying day. At his premature death at the age of 42, he left his entire estate to his former fiancée.

This story of heartbreak and love lost may seem lacking in hope. Kierkegaard himself, though, viewed his sadness through a peculiarly existentialist lens. Reflecting on his life journey, he concluded that joy was intricately linked with suffering. He described himself as, paradoxically, 'an extremely unhappy man, who nevertheless, by the help of God, is indescribably blessed'. We certainly should not revel in suffering or try to seek it out. There is nothing to be celebrated in the unforgiving and bleak nature of affliction. But, similar to Kierkegaard, my own journey through pain, anxiety and disability has taught me that there is something in suffering that can lead us to daily gratitude. It is in this sense that Aleksandr Solzhenitsyn could write of his horrific time in a Soviet Gulag: 'I lay there on rotting prison straw... I nourished my soul there, and I say without hesitation: Bless you, prison, for having been in my life.'

Solzhenitsyn, of course, was looking back at his suffering with the benefit and comfort of hindsight. In reality, embracing gratitude during times of pain and suffering is particularly demanding. When we are getting everything on our wish list, thanks and praise is easy. Gratitude when we are hurting is far more challenging. Scripture, though, implores the faithful to 'give thanks in all circumstances; for this is God's will for you in Christ Jesus' (1 Thessalonians 5:18).

Writer Elisabeth Elliot proposes that gratitude should be the defining trait of Christians in today's world. Rather than fixating on what we have or what we lack, she challenges believers to cultivate a spirit of thankfulness. Despite being no stranger to suffering herself, her life echoes this attitude. Her first husband was tragically killed by the Auca tribe in Ecuador, and her second husband died of cancer early in their marriage. Yet, Elliot decided to move with her young daughter to the rainforests of Ecuador to live among the tribe who murdered her husband. This seems an astonishing move, but she later wrote that this tribe revealed to her family the true meaning of gratitude, even amid daily struggles. In a remarkable reflection, she acknowledges that her daughter was given an extraordinary gift from the same tribe who tragically took her husband's life. This gift, which she might never have found in the western world, was a profound, enduring gratitude for life's simple, everyday blessings.

## Embracing the grace of gratitude

During my own struggle and recovery, I continued the practice I started on pilgrimage of saying 'grace' before any food I consumed. The word 'grace' in this sense is not only linked to God's unconditional and unmerited love but also comes to us from the Latin noun *gratia*, meaning 'gratitude'. The gradual loss of prayers before meals in our society, not to mention the waning of interest in the Harvest festival, has distanced us from our gratitude both to God and to others. As we receive in grace, we say 'grace' in return and, by doing so, recognise our dependency on both God and other people involved in the chain of labour that brings food to our plates.

The practice of saying 'grace' before meals is, though, only one way of adopting an attitude of gratitude in our lives. Other ways include keeping a gratitude journal, spending an examen moment of quiet reflection at the end of each day, or building gratitude into our relationships by thanking people in conversations or in phone calls and texts. Integrating practices in our life can make gratitude a natural and enduring part of our perspective. The key is to practice gratitude daily. Like manna in the desert, our gifts arrive fresh each day, even in seasons of trial, and so they demand our constant attention and appreciation.

Academic studies have consistently revealed the benefits of integrating such practices of gratitude. Those who make gratitude a natural and enduring part of daily life are, on average, happier and more fulfilled than those who do not. They are also less depressed, more generous and have a greater sense of purpose in their lives. Gratitude is a powerful emotion that draws us away from the traps of self-sufficiency and self-absorption. It helps us acknowledge our dependence on others and recognise that what we have in life is not earned by our own efforts but is graciously given.

Philosopher Michael Sandel suggests that the fourth-century Augustine–Pelagius debate over whether salvation is rooted in grace or human effort has echoes in today's meritocratic culture. Critiquing the 'tyranny of merit' that dominates modern society, Sandel argues that our individualistic pride convinces us we fully deserve what we have. He therefore calls for a recovery of 'mutual indebtedness', encouraging us to embrace humility and gratitude for the gifts of family, community and country.

As gratitude grows in our lives, we begin to recognise how dependent we are on many people in so many ways. This recognition of our dependence *on* others inspires us to reach out *to* others. Life, after all, is a beautiful balance of receiving and giving. After his cancer diagnosis, while facing his final few months, the author and neurologist Oliver Sacks reflected on his life. In recognising the profound interconnectedness of human existence, he wrote about the constant flow of dependence in his past – there were times when he had leaned on others, just as there were times when others had leaned on him. He concluded: 'My predominant feeling is one of gratitude. I have loved and been loved. I have been given much and I have given something in return.'

Moved by gratitude for what we have received from others, we naturally give back, often without even realising the profound impact our contributions have on the lives of those around us. In the 2002 film *About Schmidt*, the eponymous character, played by Jack Nicholson, spends the entire film grappling with a haunting sense of insignificance. He questions whether his life has mattered at all, convinced that, soon enough, it will be as though he never existed. In a moving final scene, though, Schmidt opens a letter from Ndugu, a six-year-old Tanzanian child he has been sponsoring and to which he has been writing. The child informs him how much his letters and financial support have been appreciated. Despite the fact they had never met, he also includes a simple crayon drawing of him holding hands with Schmidt on a sunny day. Tears start to flow from the eyes of the usually detached and reserved Schmidt, as he becomes aware that he is part of a life-enhancing, mutual exchange of giving-and-receiving love. Entitlement and ingratitude cut us off from this powerful flow. When we affirm this shared flow of love, though, we can lift our communities, inspire our society and enrich our own lives with greater health, happiness and fulfilment.

This process takes on a deeper and more profound meaning when we recognise the ultimate source of all gifts – someone we are utterly dependent upon and who gives to us out of love. While the emotional and psychological benefits of gratitude are undeniable, something vital feels absent without a greater presence to whom our gratitude is directed. As agnostic author Douglas Coupland puts it: 'I need God, because without God I can't say "thank you" to anyone, without God I can't say sorry to anyone, without God I can't truly love.' Distinguishing between gratitude and thankfulness can be helpful. Gratitude is about appreciating *what* we've received, while thankfulness directs that appreciation towards *who* gave it. In this way, for Christians, gratitude naturally deepens into thankfulness, connecting us to the ultimate giver. 'The gift', writes theologian Graham Tomlin, 'becomes something richer – a sign of a greater love, a deeper reality behind the gift itself.'

Through the struggle of my second pilgrimage, I discovered that directing my thankfulness towards God further illuminated the final cornerstone of my journey – hope. This hope was not merely a fleeting feeling. It was the rock that anchored both of my pilgrimages, holding me steady through every step. As I wrestled with pain, sinking into the familiar comfort of my red sofa, a friend sat beside me and spoke words that will forever link gratitude and hope in my heart. Their wisdom stayed with me long beyond my recovery. 'Look back and thank God,' he said; 'look forward and trust God.'

## TIME TO REFLECT

- How deeply is gratitude woven into the journeys you are on right now?

- What simple practices could help you become more mindful of the gifts God has given and the love others have shown you – like taking time to reflect, writing down moments of thankfulness or saying a quiet prayer of thanks each day?

- How might your gratitude flow outward by offering your time, encouragement or presence to support others on their own paths?

# 6

# Hope

*Pilgrimage exists to help us remember the mysteries you forgot at home.*

Phil Cousineau, filmmaker

*Our painful experiences aren't a liability – they're a gift. They give us perspective and meaning, an opportunity to find our unique purpose and our strength.*

Edith Eger, holocaust survivor

## JOURNEY ONE: PILGRIM'S WAY

## Getting to the end

The Russian novelist Ivan Turgenev once suggested that everyone should write the story of their life before leaving this world. My grandmother went some way in doing just that, leaving us beautifully handwritten diaries filled with captivating tales of her youth. Writing this book is likely to be the closest I will come to my own autobiography. Yet it captures only a single year out of my half-century on this planet, a fleeting moment in the grand scheme of things. It was, though, a year that profoundly shaped me, challenging me in ways I never expected – physically, emotionally and spiritually.

My walk on the Pilgrim's Way was part of a sabbatical from ministry, so before I left, my bishop requested that I justify the 'purpose' of the walk. 'There has to be a reason that you are crazy enough to walk 140 miles!', as she put it, rather starkly and sharply. Having been put on the spot, I struggled to answer eloquently and simply said: 'Well, I suppose the purpose is to get to the end of the journey.' The answer may have lacked inspiration, but it was understandable. Many of our journeys only make sense in hindsight, when we can look back at the highs and lows of our travels. Kierkegaard famously wrote that 'the secret of all existence is movement'. Of course, I knew my pilgrimage would involve plenty of physical movement – long, demanding daily walks, progressing from one point on the map to the next overnight stop. But on pilgrimage, movement is not just about the body. The journey is as much about spiritual growth and personal transformation as it is about covering miles. At its heart, pilgrimage is a movement towards God.

Before pilgrims are able to reflect on travels with hindsight, though, simply 'getting to the end' is an appropriate intention. After all, pilgrimage is usually a journey to a particular place that is considered unique or sacred. One of the greatest challenges on the Pilgrim's Way is reaching the destination, with unpredictable weather often preventing pilgrims from completing the journey. Ferry crossings to Ynys Enlli (Bardsey Island) are frequently cancelled due to rough seas and powerful currents. Fittingly, the name 'Ynys Enlli' even means 'Island of Currents'. For many, this means the bittersweet frustration of having to abandon the final leg of their journey, leaving the pilgrimage unfinished despite coming so close.

## Ynys Enlli (Bardsey Island)

In her book *Wayfarer*, Phoebe Smith recounts the disappointment of walking the whole of the Pilgrim's Way but not making it to Ynys Enlli, as she was told the rough seas might not calm for weeks. Her journey stopped short, but I was fortunate. Despite enduring torrential rain at times, I arrived at Porth Meudwy in glorious sunshine, gazing out over a crystalline sea. Porth Meudwy means 'Hermit's Port' and it has long been a gateway to Enlli, its history stretching back centuries. As I boarded the small ferry for the 40-minute crossing, I felt a profound sense of peace wash over me. Enlli has been revered for generations and has a reputation as one of Wales' 'thin places', where the boundary between earth and heaven feels blurred. *The Book of Llandaff* (1120) calls it the 'Rome of Britain' and claims that 20,000 saints are buried on its sacred soil. So significant was the island in pre-Reformation times that three pilgrimages to Enlli were considered equivalent to one journey to Rome. Contemplating its wonder from the ferry, I began to understand why.

Pilgrims down the ages have been drawn to this island for its bleak remoteness, far from our usual daily concerns. Recently, the island has become as serene and hermitic as ever, with its population falling from 132 in the 19th century to just 4 in a recent census. As I disembarked from the ferry, I felt I was stepping onto sacred ground. After an eventful 140-mile walk, I had to stop myself from falling on to my painful knees and kissing the ground, as Pope John Paul II would famously do when visiting new countries. As I roamed the island, in the company of only the seals resting on the beaches, I felt the tranquillity of the landscape seep into my spirit, bringing with it a profound sense of inner peace. The Welsh have a word for this kind of deep, soul-soothing harmony – *tangnefedd*. In that moment, I experienced its fullness, a calm so deep it carried with it an unmistakable sense of hope. The challenges and triumphs of my three-week walk had changed me in ways I could not yet fully articulate, but I knew one thing for certain – I was leaving this place with a small but precious kernel of hope, ready to be cherished and nurtured.

Reaching Enlli brought with it a powerful sense of accomplishment, but, in the spirit of pilgrimage, arriving is only part of the journey. The Nobel-nominated poet R.S. Thomas, once the parish priest of Aberdaron, the village where pilgrims traditionally pause before crossing to Enlli, captures this idea in his poem 'Migrants'. For Thomas, the ultimate aim of travel is not to reach the destination. Instead, he likens the journey to gathering pollen in our minds, which we can later transform into the sweet, sustaining honey of insight and renewal upon our return home.

## Kingdom flowers

R.S. Thomas' perspective resonates deeply with the biblical narrative. In the Old Testament, the nomadic Israelites worshipped their pilgrim God in a tent, carrying a physical reminder of his presence in the ark of the covenant. When God became man, journeying remained central to the story of salvation. From Jesus' earliest days, movement shaped his life, with his travelling to Bethlehem, fleeing to Egypt and settling in Nazareth. As an adult, his ministry unfolded on the road, the path of a homeless wanderer bringing the good news to all who would listen. 'Foxes have dens and birds have nests,' he tells his disciples, 'but the Son of Man has nowhere to lay his head' (Matthew 8:20). So, the God of the Bible is the God of the journey. Thus, in the experiences of our own travels, we connect with something of the ultimate and eternal. These experiences stretch beyond our normal day-to-day lives and, if we allow them, can begin to mould and transform us, shaping our thinking, assumptions and beliefs. As Charles Foster puts it: 'As the kingdom sprang up around the sandals of Jesus, so kingdom flowers can spring up around pilgrim boots.'

The 'kingdom flowers' of pilgrimage continue to bloom in our souls long after we have returned home. These blossoms are the uplifting moments of the walk that linger in us as we return to our everyday lives – the awe of nature's grandeur, profound connections with fellow travellers, and moments of connection and coincidence. But they also include something quieter yet equally powerful. This is what Tolstoy in *War and Peace* calls 'the satisfaction of simple human needs'. On the Pilgrim's Way, these were the small joys that brought a surprising depth of contentment – the salty tang of fresh air on a sea cliff walk, the burst of sweetness from raisins during an especially gruelling stretch, the luxury of a warm bath infused with relaxing salts after a long day hiking, the softness of clean sheets as sleep embraced me at night, and putting on dry clothes each morning. These moments, though simple, transformed the mundane into something deeply meaningful.

Yet, paradoxically, the 'kingdom flowers' of pilgrimage are not only born from moments of joy or satisfaction. By the time my walk drew to a close, I had come to understand that the times of intense struggle and hardship also hold their own sacred power, offering profound encounters with God. These experiences shape and transform us just as deeply as the moments of delight. After all, the life-giving journeys in the Bible are demanding and difficult, from the wanderings of Abraham and Jacob to the exodus and exile. Jesus' journey to the cross was similarly gruelling, and he instructed his followers to expect their journeys to be as arduous, encouraging them to tread in his footsteps on the tortuous *Via Dolorosa* ('Way of Suffering'): 'Whoever wants to be my disciple must deny themselves and take up their cross and follow me' (Matthew 16:24).

## Our cyclical lives

In facing both the joys and challenges of their travels, pilgrims often begin to view their journeys, and subsequently life in general, as cyclical. For the final few days on the Pilgrim's Way, walkers are treated to the breathtaking views from the Llŷn Peninsula cliffs. Each day I would sit on a cliff edge gazing out at the Irish Sea with my sandwiches and my trusty flask of tea, contemplating the natural ebb and flow in the rhythm of the tide. It brought to mind the highs and lows of my journey, but also the ebb and flow of life. The storms of suffering often sweep into our lives like a raging tide. At those moments, though, we can reassure ourselves that this suffering will soon retreat, giving way to more uplifting and buoyant moments. Likewise, even in our most joyous moments, we know that suffering is not far away and could puncture our bliss at any time. Rather than being a depressing thought, this brought comfort to my journey. The sixth-century theologian Boethius describes life as a wheel:

We rise up on the spokes but we're soon cast back down into the depths. Good times pass away, but then so do the bad. Change is our tragedy, but it's also our hope. The worst of times, like the best, are always passing away.

So, we make peace with our journeys of constant change. When we are content and comfortable, we embrace the knowledge it is temporary. When we are anxious or in despair, we embrace the knowledge it will pass. 'Weeping may stay for the night,' as the psalmist put it, 'but rejoicing comes in the morning' (Psalm 30:5).

One of the most often-quoted passages in the Old Testament similarly reassures us of the tidal motion of our journeys. In Ecclesiastes 3:1–8, the writer uses a popular rabbinic literary technique to describe the transience of events, emotions and activities. 'There is a time for everything, and a season for every activity under the heavens', he states in the first line of this beautiful passage. The writer is reminding us of the reality of the human condition – that all of us experience both suffering *and* joy, anxiety *and* peace, despair *and* hope. According to Kierkegaard, part of the wonderful paradox of the Christian faith is that it accepts the coexistence of both light and shadow in our lives. After all, Jesus was the ultimate blessing to those who loved him. Yet that blessing did not save his mother from heart-wrenching grief nor his disciples from bloody martyrdom. Neither did his divinity and perfect humanity save him from his own grief, pain, anxiety, torture and death. And so, Kierkegaard maintains, Jesus 'understands all your sorrow better than you understand it yourself'. This is the ultimate reassurance when the ebb and flow of life leads us to times of suffering, anxiety and despair.

## Absolute availability

Like our lives, pilgrimages are ever-evolving and ever-changing. Ultimately, the challenge is for us to embrace both the peaks and troughs as an opportunity to cultivate our capacity for compassion and care for ourselves and others. It is through our openness to experiences, people and events that hope is birthed. Philosopher Gabriel Marcel emphasises the vital role of 'availability' in our lives. He defines this as a readiness to devote ourselves fully to life, describing it as 'the aptitude to give oneself to anything which offers, and to bind oneself by the gift'. In contrast, our default state often leans towards self-preoccupation and self-absorption, where we view others and situations simply as means of fulfilling our own desires. However, through genuine availability, we shift our perspective and become fully receptive, responsive and open to the needs and existence of others.

Friends of mine describe how the unexpected shock of a birth of a child with a disability did not destroy their dreams of the perfect family. Rather, it allowed them to love in ways they never thought possible. And so the child became a blessing to them and others, just as they became a blessing to their child. Thus, 'availability' invites us to open our hearts, allowing us to both give and receive freely. We become a gift to others, just as they become a gift to us. Marcel suggests that the ultimate goal is to attain *disponibilité absolue* ('absolute availability'), a state where our kindness and generosity extend beyond our family and friends, reaching even those with whom we share no immediate connection. In this way, our lives become a blessing to all.

Theologian Khaled Anatolios roots Marcel's 'availability' in the Trinity. The Spirit is the heartbeat of the gift we offer to, and receive from, others, but it is through the relationship between the Son and the Father that the concept can speak most tangibly to our daily lives. 'I have given them the glory that you gave me,' Jesus said, 'that they may be one as we are one – I in them and you in me – so that they may be brought to complete unity' (John 17:22–23). The mutual reciprocity of the incarnation came alive as I trod the ancient paths of the pilgrimage. I found myself both seeing Jesus in those I encountered and being Jesus to them, from the bird watchers I shared my lunch with on the slopes of Eryri (Snowdonia) to the tourists I laughed with outside Bangor Cathedral.

The 19th-century philosopher Hegel argued that the 'truth' of the Christian faith unfolded over two millennia. Pilgrimage reminds us that this unfolding continues in our own lives. Through the daily highs and lows, as we learn to give and receive love, we are drawn ever closer to the ultimate source of that love.

## Walk on

My time on the hallowed ground of Ynys Enlli at the end of the pilgrimage was only a brief six hours. It was, though, long enough for me to reflect on the journey's ups and downs. The pilgrimage had been a beautifully life-affirming escape from the demands of my daily grind. It was a chance to step away from the constant push to succeed and the gnawing need for approval. In the wilderness of pilgrimage, I found liberation from fear and insecurity.

Yet the wilderness of the journey had its shadow side too. Alongside the sense of freedom came moments of loneliness, fear and pain. At those times, I was reminded of the actor and martial arts expert Bruce Lee, who stated that, when he was frightened or scared, he would repeat to himself, over and over again: 'Walk on, Bruce; walk on, Bruce.' There were times on the pilgrimage when all I could do was keep walking on.

As I sat on the ferry returning from Ynys Enlli, I had no idea the curveball life was about to throw. I did know, though, that I had already been through a metamorphic experience. Kierkegaard suggests that all journeys are bookended by a withdrawal from the world and a return to the world. For him, the ultimate archetype of this was the pilgrimage of Abraham on Mount Moriah, where his only son Isaac is given a last-minute reprieve from being sacrificed horrifically (Genesis 22:1–19). Many Christians struggle with a story of God demanding that a loving father commits infanticide, only to stop the slaughter at the last moment. The *Los Angeles Times* reports that, not only do Christians wish this story did not exist in the Bible, but many prominent Jewish and Islamic thinkers also have grave reservations about the narrative. After all, it seems horrifying that God demands a human sacrifice, while Abraham's servile compliance is incomprehensible. In the words of James Goodman, a finalist for the Pulitzer Prize, the whole episode is 'evidence that God is a tyrant, Abraham a sycophant, and both of them abusers of poor Isaac'.

For Kierkegaard, though, to over-concern ourselves with the morality of the Moriah narrative misses its depth. Traditionally, he writes, Christians have failed to recognise the importance of the story's resolution, when Abraham simply returns to his daily life. This homecoming back to an everyday existence is as important as his initial withdrawal to Mount Moriah. He returns profoundly challenged and changed, with a new-found gratitude for God's earthly gifts. Not that Kierkegaard views this story through rose-tinted spectacles. He criticises any focus on a happy ending to the patriarch's trial. Abraham does gain something precious on the slopes of Moriah, but the harrowing trauma of his ordeal is immense. He does find spiritual solace, but only after a journey which plumbed the depths of pain and distress. This, claims Kierkegaard, reflects the paradox of the Christian journey – pilgrimage is costly, but the rewards are great. 'Only the one who is in anxiety finds rest,' he concludes, 'only the one who draws the knife gets Isaac.'

Before returning to Cardiff after finishing the Pilgrim's Way, I stayed the night at my parents' house in North Wales. As I talked to my mum in her cozy living room, I gazed out the window. There, stretching across the majestic Conwy Mountain, was the most radiant, crystal-clear rainbow I had ever seen. Reflecting on the rainbow's significance in the Noahic covenant (Genesis 9:13–16), it felt as though God was whispering promises of renewal and hope into my heart. I could not resist rushing outside to capture the moment. When I turned back, I saw my mother standing at the window, her face lit with a warm smile, while the rainbow reflected beautifully on the glass. I snapped a photo, not realising the deep significance it would later hold. During the Covid pandemic, when visiting elderly loved ones was limited to waving through windows, that image became a poignant symbol of grace for our family. At the time, though, I simply embraced the rainbow as a sign of hope. This hope was to carry me forward after an eventful pilgrimage and would continue to shine through the challenges of my second, equally transformative journey.

## JOURNEY TWO: THROUGH INJURY AND DARKNESS

## Two similar but different journeys

Traditionally, those undertaking pilgrimages accept that difficulty, uncertainty and ordeal will be part of the journey. Sometimes danger is positively embraced. In his BBC series *Extreme Pilgrim*, Peter Owen-Jones explored the challenging journeys people of faith have undertaken down the years. He even re-enacted some of the most extreme examples of spiritual discipline. In one episode, he considers the desert fathers of the third-century ancient Near East. In particular, he followed the footsteps of the ascetic St Anthony the Great, who spent his final 43 years in a hermit cave in the primordial landscape of the Egyptian desert. Under the stewardship of Father Lazarus El Anthony, a contemporary Coptic hermit, Owen-Jones was taken to an isolated cave in the wilderness and there spent 21 taxing days in extreme heat and solitude.

This was a much more extreme undertaking than my North Wales pilgrimage. However, like Owen-Jones, from the very beginning I knew my journey would test me, and I welcomed this as part of its purpose. On my second pilgrimage, the challenge was different. This time, there was no choice. Instead, I was cast head-first into a journey I neither planned nor wanted. My first journey could therefore be described as created isolation and challenge, while the second was enforced isolation and challenge. Though these two journeys were very different, both pushed me to confront profound and sobering truths. Whether walking the Pilgrim's Way or grappling with pain on my sofa, both experiences compelled me to wrestle with deep questions about belief, faith, identity and mortality. These questions demanded reflection and response, and ultimately they resulted in growth and transformation.

## Finding God and finding ourselves

Philosopher Charles Foster suggests that every pilgrimage is 'a kind of rebirth' which profoundly transforms the pilgrim. Hope would come to shape my second journey, but in the beginning, I felt only isolation, wandering through a barren landscape of worry and pain. The feeling of abandonment in a wilderness is, of course, thoroughly biblical. Nearly every major figure in scripture undergoes a desert experience. For some, like Abraham, Moses and Jesus, the desert is literal. For others, like Jonah in the belly of the whale or Paul during his temporary blindness, the wilderness is more symbolic. Yet for all of them, the isolation and challenge of the desert becomes a sacred space for preparation, prayer and transformation. These profound encounters even lead to new identities, with Abram becoming Abraham and Saul being reborn as Paul. The desert, whether physical or spiritual, is where God shapes his people for what lies ahead.

Not that such wilderness journeys are uniquely Christian. In his seminal work on the myth of the hero, Joseph Campbell notes that patriarchs, gods and heroes undergo the same process in other faiths and cultures, with characters leaving the security and domesticity of home to embark on the challenge of a desert experience. This has, of course, been translated into contemporary myths, from Luke Skywalker in *Star Wars: A New Hope* to Katniss Everdeen in *The Hunger Games*. As the title of the first Star Wars film intimates, it is in these wilderness experiences that hope is birthed, as inchoate strengths are developed and obstacles are overcome.

All this, though, was scant reassurance as I whiled away my days at home, even struggling to embark on short daily walks without considerable pain. This was a lonely and frustrating journey. It is difficult to believe that God redeems the wasteland, leaving nothing to waste, when you feel forsaken in its arid emptiness. In the book of Exodus, Moses took his sheep 'to the far side of the wilderness' (Exodus 3:1) to escape execution after killing an Egyptian guard. The early Jewish rabbinic tradition elaborates on this narrative, describing a small lamb escaping from Moses' flock. Moses pursues the creature, but as the lamb is unusually nimble, Moses is forced further and further into the wilderness. It is in the deepest, darkest area of the desert that he experiences Yahweh in the burning bush. Here also he finally catches his lively little lamb. The early rabbis explain that the lamb represents Moses' own inmost self. It took, therefore, a journey deep into the wilderness to discover both himself and his God.

The dominant ethos in the west today is centred around identity – a championing of personal freedom and authenticity. This leads to a belief that our journeys revolve around our individual selves. The concept of 'finding ourselves' has become overused and self-indulgent. Yet the early rabbis would have had an entirely different perspective on what it means to find ourselves. They taught that Moses would not have found the lamb without also finding the burning bush. In other words, by 'finding himself' he discovered that life was not about his own desires and ego. Rather, life was about his God-given vocation to serve and love. This profound realisation, though, was not a straightforward discovery for the patriarch. Rather, it required a journey through bleak and ruthless wilderness. Or as theologian Joan Chittister puts it: 'There is a light in us that only darkness itself can illuminate.'

## Nothing, nothing, nothing

At some point in life, each of us will be thrust into a journey through an unforgiving desert. Whether it is illness, grief, unemployment, depression or another hardship, these arid seasons test us deeply. My own wilderness came in the form of the excruciating pain that followed my pilgrimage, leaving me largely confined to my sofa. Recovery was a slow and exhausting process, often feeling like I was once again trudging through the viscous mud of North Wales. Yet, the true nature of wilderness is not defined by our outward circumstances. Instead, it lies in the inner battles we face, the internal struggles that shape and challenge us in ways we never imagined. Those inhospitable and lonely places are inside of us, as we plumb the depths of despair. Through this, we are stripped bare, our flaws and vulnerabilities laid painfully clear for all to see.

On our journeys through barren land, God can seem conspicuously absent. In the early days of Celtic Christianity, monastics would talk of the monsters and demons they encountered on mountaintops and isolated islands. 'It is not all angels and doves when pushing into the wilderness', warns Nick Mayhew-Smith. In forcing us to face our vulnerability, the desert strips away our comfortable lives and leaves us unmoored, struggling to make sense of our predicament. Here we find another of the great pilgrimage paradoxes. God meets us in those moments when he seems most distant. Martin Luther pictures God working *sub contrario* ('under the appearance of the opposite'). Thus, he is most fully present when he feels absent, his light most dazzling when we are lost in the dark, his strength most comforting when we feel weak, and his power most reassuring when we are forced to relinquish our own attempts to control.

Inspired by the desert fathers of the east, the early Celtic Christians were acutely aware of this paradox. Despite the bleakness of the wilderness places through which they travelled, experiences of the divine were at the heart of their journeys. These early Welsh monastics retreated to places that were outside of social structures and networks, such as caves, mountaintops or remote islands like Enlli, to connect with their God.

While a red sofa is nowhere as romantic or mysterious as wild Welsh countryside, I still found myself utterly reliant on God. Gripping tightly to a small wooden Palestinian cross a friend had given me many years earlier, God was the rock and hope that I clung to, despite how distant he sometimes felt. St John of the Cross' words 'nothing, nothing, nothing' became important to me in my recovery. I would repeat those words ('*nada, nada, nada*'), slowly and thoughtfully, reminding myself that my ultimate worth was in God and only his presence mattered. Suffering strips us of the need for esteem, wealth, affirmation, and even affection, as our human attachments and desires fall away. We are left with 'nothing, nothing, nothing', other than his love which fills our hearts and his light which illuminates those things that really matter in our lives. 'In God's boundless and relentless love for us,' writes Richard Rice, 'God refuses to let our sufferings just lie there, unmitigated and unredeemed.'

## The unbearable weight of regret

The reassuring knowledge of God's love and presence, though, does not shield us from the ravages of the wilderness journey. For me, the silence of that journey led to an intrusive thought that lingered during the day and kept me up at night. This recurring thought was centred on regret. My mind kept grappling with the question of why I went on the North Wales pilgrimage in the first place and, indeed, why I didn't abandon the walk when severe tendonitis struck my knee. The Pilgrim's Way had brought incredible blessings, yet I could not ignore the harsh reality that my second journey, marked by pain and injury, was the direct consequence of choices I had naively made during that fateful first trek.

Yet I soon came to recognise that 'what if?' is a futile question. It introduces itself as innocent reflection but soon overwhelms us. Regret, after all, is a way of trying to control both the past and the future. It is, ultimately, damaging to our recovery. It is human nature to want to take charge of situations and steer events in our favour. When we feel control slipping away, our brain's amygdala kicks into gear, triggering fear and anxiety as if sounding an internal alarm. I have long been obsessed with books, films and TV series about time travel – *Back to the Future*, *12 Monkeys*, *The Time Traveller's Wife* and so on. There is something captivating about the idea of travelling back in time to rewrite the present or leaping forward for reassurance that everything will work out. But, however appealing the fantasy might be, control can never truly be ours to hold.

In *Room of Marvels*, James Bryan Smith shares a profound dream he had while grappling with the grief of losing his mother, best friend and daughter in quick succession. In the dream, he is taken to heaven, where his best friend insists that he rides a horse while facing backwards. Everything in Smith's instincts screams that riding backwards is reckless, yet his friend urges him to trust the horse to guide the journey. 'By riding backwards, you won't be able to see where you're going,' his friend explains; 'you will know you have surrendered control when you can do that with joy.' Smith draws a parallel to scripture, pointing to the Virgin Mary as the ultimate example of surrender. At the annunciation, Mary chose to let go of fear and fully trust in God's plan. In stark contrast, King Saul's downfall in the Old Testament stemmed from his refusal to relinquish control over his life. Smith concludes that these examples reveal a profound truth – surrendering control leads us away from regret and towards God's promise of joy and hope.

Edith Eger carried the heavy burden of regret for decades following her harrowing incarceration at Auschwitz. She recounts the moment she stepped off the cattle carriage after an excruciating journey, only to come face-to-face with the infamous Dr Mengele. When he asked the 16-year-old Eger whether the woman beside her was her sister, she instinctively replied that it was her mother. With those words, her mother was sent to the other queue – the one that led to the gas chambers. Eger became consumed by the weight of that moment, her regret gnawing at her for decades. 'I should have said "sister"! Why didn't I say "sister"? I call to her across the years, to ask her forgiveness', she wrote years later.

Her litany of guilt and regret held her back for many years until, in the 1960s, she struck up a friendship with fellow Auschwitz-survivor Viktor Frankl. Through his influence, she began to view her journey through the lens of 'choice'. For her own well-being and the good of others, she decided to set aside the choice she made as a scared and hungry 16-year-old. Instead, she chose to embrace herself fully, flaws and all, as perfectly imperfect and deeply human. 'I can't ever change the past,' she writes. 'But there is a life I can save: it is mine. The one I am living right now, this precious moment.' Eger went on to develop a powerful therapeutic approach known as 'choice therapy', designed to help free those trapped in the prisons of regret and guilt, offering a path towards healing and liberation.

During my second pilgrimage of recovery, Eger's inspiring work challenged me to break free from the endless cycle of 'if only I hadn't' and start moving forward. Drowning in 'what-ifs' was not only stalling my recovery but also distancing me from the people I loved. I had become a prisoner of my own regrets, locked inside a cell of my own making. Even when I shifted my focus to looking forward to a future when my back would be healed, I realised I was still enslaved, chained to a distant hope that kept me from truly living in the present. It was not until I surrendered control back to God and embraced my current reality, however bleak it felt, that I began to experience healing, hope and the liberating power of acceptance. Eger concludes: 'Freedom means we must muster the courage to dismantle the prison, brick by brick.'

# ON OUR JOURNEYS

## Exile, restoration and resurrection

Gaining this liberation in our journeys can be a long process with many setbacks. Our time in the wilderness resembles the long Jewish exile in Babylon, where the Israelites lost their familiar environment and had to forge a new identity and meaning. Here they faced struggle and tears, helplessness and hopelessness, and a longing to go back to the way things used to be. 'By the rivers of Babylon we sat and wept when we remembered Zion', as Psalm 137 puts it.

Anyone who endures chronic pain, whether from disc degeneration and prolapse, as in my case, or from conditions like chronic fatigue, arthritis or MS, knows how relentless and draining it can be. For most people, energy is a resource that carries them comfortably through the day. But for those living with chronic pain, grief or emotional turmoil, energy is finite. Even something as routine as taking a shower can deplete reserves, leaving little energy for the basic tasks of daily life. As such, the fundamental questions we ask each day change. Questions such as 'How can I be happy today?' or 'How can I have fun today?' seem unrealistic, empty and futile. The only question we ask as we struggle out of bed each morning is 'How can I avoid more pain?' No wonder the memories of our lives before pain, grief, disability or depression can haunt our dreams at night and weigh heavy on our minds during the day.

Yet, as in the Babylonian exile, we can find ourselves searching for new hope in our wilderness experiences. In my own experience, that which had long given coherence and structure to my life was lost. As I adjusted to my situation, it pushed me to re-evaluate who I was, where I stood on my life's journey, and what truly deserved my time and attention. As with the Old Testament exile, it is when everything lies in tatters that hope arises. After all, as disruptive as it is, calamity can allow an opportunity for reflection and, ultimately, growth. Despite my tendency to catastrophise, I held on to the sure and certain hope that the new life of spring would thaw the cold of winter, the light of dawn would pierce the darkness of night, and new birth would break through the bleakness of the wilderness. In his poem 'Threshold', R.S. Thomas suggests that when we are laid low by life's slings and arrows, there is often only one action that is left to us – to stretch out our hand into the dark, like Michaelangelo's Adam, trusting that we will feel a reciprocating touch of reassurance and hope.

This hope lies at the very heart of all pilgrimages. The head of Ynys Enlli points eastward, as if in anticipation of Christ's second coming, and the medieval Welsh poet Meilyr Brydydd celebrates the island as a place of glorious resurrection. In his poem 'Marwysgafn', he entrusts himself to God, longing for his body to rest among the 20,000 saints buried there, to rise with them at the resurrection. Even in the midst of struggles, pilgrimages have a way of affirming that promise of new life. During my journey of recovery, I caught fleeting glimpses of resurrection as a living, breathing reality, despite it often feeling just beyond my reach. After all, resurrection is never immediate. We must first pass through the pain of Good Friday and the silence of Holy Saturday before we can stand in the light and life of Easter Sunday.

## Embracing our marks and scars

As I lay on my red sofa for hour upon hour, day upon day, week upon week, I visualised myself wrestling with God, like Jacob in the book of Genesis (32:22–32). Frustrated and in pain, I found myself pleading for a speedy recovery, only to grow exasperated when reality refused to meet my demands. The significance of Jacob's wrestle with God, though, lies as much with the narrative's resolution as it does with the event itself. At the end of the passage, Jacob is given new purpose and fresh motivation to continue his journey. He does so, though, having been physically scarred through his experience. His wrestle, after all, left him limping from a dislocated hip. Coincidentally, my own suffering also included excruciating sciatic pain in my hip. I began to feel an affinity with Jacob and his limp. He would have been left with both constant agitation and chronic pain. But the sign of his struggle became his strength and would inspire him and countless others in the future.

Like Jacob, we all live with our own particular limps. 'My marks and scars I carry with me', Mr Valiant-for-Truth asserts in John Bunyan's *Pilgrim's Progress*. My children have always been intrigued by the scar on my back, a reminder of the titanium bolt inserted between my vertebrae 18 years ago to save my damaged disc. But the deepest and most painful scars in our lives are not physical. Whether visible or hidden, whether etched on the body or the heart, our scars are not wasted in God's hands. Through him, our wilderness experiences equip us with the compassion and strength to support others navigating their own deserts. Suffering may scar us, but God transforms it into a tool for love, care and healing. 'The most beautiful stones', writes James Bryan Smith, 'are the ones that have been tossed by the wind and washed by the water and polished to brilliance by life's strongest storms.'

My own spinal condition has stopped me from living life fully ever since my early 30s, and I am unlikely to be free of its weighty burden. Long before the relapse that followed my pilgrimage, I dreamed of waking up one day free from chronic pain and the fatigue of pacing my life just to manage it. Yet, in the wake of my relapse, I have come to see something unexpected. My pain has been a strange, paradoxical gift. It is certainly not a gift I would have chosen, but it is one that has profoundly shaped me. During my road of recovery, one parishioner visited and encouraged me to learn to love my back, which seemed almost absurd at the time. She suggested that I make time each day to recite a meditation that she had composed. This began with forgiving my body for letting me down and forgiving my spine for its weakness. It then went on to an acceptance of my present predicament, choosing to love my body, just as it is, and love myself, just as I am. Finally, I would commit to embracing with hope and expectation the future that God held for me. Likewise, in all our journeys, whatever we are facing, we can meet the present with grace, the past with compassion and the road ahead with hope.

## Weaving a new harmony

The raw journey of my second pilgrimage helped me to recognise that, while God does not want us to suffer, he can transform our struggles entirely. In *The Silmarillion*, the backstory to *The Lord of the Rings*, Tolkien presents his own vision of creation, in which God brings the universe into being through the sweet and harmonious singing of angels.

Before long, a rebellious and flawed angel breaks away, singing out of tune in a desperate attempt to sow discord and chaos. Yet God, in his infinite wisdom, does not silence the dissonance. Instead, he weaves a new harmony around it, transforming even the discordant notes into something beautiful. In this way, even the recalcitrant angel's fall from grace is ultimately drawn into God's higher purposes.

Similarly, God is deeply affected by the discord in our own lives and he works to redeem and restore harmony. There is no passivity to suffering where God is concerned. He inspires creative and resourceful responses to the situations that befall us. At a superficial level, the apostle Paul's assertion that 'all things work together for good to those who love God' (Romans 8:28, NKJV) may seem glib and even untrue. After all, many who love God suffer appallingly. However, this passage does not imply that the faithful are immune to life's trials. Rather, it is affirming the truth that God works for good in the midst of life's setbacks and hurts. Whatever storms we face, God is moving to promote growth and fullness of life.

When Michael J. Fox was diagnosed with young-onset Parkinson's at the age of 29, his world imploded. Yet, since then, he has brought hope to so many through his inspirational books and his tireless charity work, including establishing a foundation that has collected $1 billion for medical research. In reflecting on his life since his devastating diagnoses, he concludes: 'Good things can come from bad things.' As a Christian, the truth that God works through our suffering is a central truth that affirms this axiom. Despite the dehumanising nature of pain, we can still recognise that God brings good through even the most hopeless and helpless moments, as Jesus' death and resurrection affirms. No wonder the apostle Paul writes that we can 'glory in our sufferings' (Romans 5:3). It is through suffering that hope is realised.

In 2006, the year I was recovering from major back surgery, a young woman in my city was facing her own unimaginable tragedy. With a five-year-old son and a newborn daughter, she lost her husband to an aggressive cancer. Over the next five years, she walked the path of grief while I navigated the challenges of chronic pain and disability. It was during this time of healing and struggle that our paths crossed and we fell in love. We were soon married in a celebration filled with hope and joy. We are both deeply aware that if we had not endured those separate journeys of suffering, we might never have found the extraordinary gift of our marriage. Neither would I have had the profound privilege of loving, and being loved by, two remarkable children. And then, as if grace could not be outdone, our family grew with the arrival of another gift – a son and little brother, bringing boundless joy to us all.

Miroslav Volf, reflecting on his own profound journey through loss and pain, from the heartbreak of infertility to the joy of adoption, captured it beautifully when he wrote: 'Since it gave me what I now can't imagine living without, poison was transmuted into a gift, God's strange gift. The pain of it remains, of course. But the poison is gone.' Through the shattered shards of our lives, God creates a glorious mosaic.

## TIME TO REFLECT

- Think back to the chapters of your life when God brought beauty, healing or hope out of even the most difficult places. Are there wounds that have become sources of strength or moments of struggle that have deepened your compassion for others?

- In your current journeys, where have you seen God quietly at work for good, even in the darkest or most difficult moments?

# Epilogue

*Something very beautiful happens to people when their world has fallen apart: a humility, a nobility, a higher intelligence emerges just at that point when our knees hit the floor.*

Marianne Williamson, author and political activist

*As human beings, you have to understand that adversity is part of your life, and, when it happens, you find yourself.*

Alex Ferguson, reflecting on his football management career and his recovery from a brain haemorrhage, in the film *Sir Alex Ferguson: Never Give In* (2021)

## Sunshine and shadows

There are so many spectacular views that stop pilgrims in their tracks on the Pilgrim's Way. My favourite view was at the halfway point of the trail. But this breathtaking panorama came as no surprise to me. It was a view that I would gaze at daily as a child, growing up in Penmaenmawr on the North Wales coast. As pilgrims advance over the mountain behind my hometown, ambling past the wonderful 'druid's circle', a stone circle dating from neolithic times, they are met with a spectacular sea view which looks directly over to Ynys Seiriol (Puffin Island).

Ynys Seiriol is situated off the east coast of Ynys Môn, the isle of Anglesey. Off its west coast, over 30 miles away, is Ynys Cybi (Holy Island), with Holyhead as its largest town. These two small islands were named after Seiriol Wyn and Cybi Felyn, who were Celtic monks who lived on their respective islands around 1,500 years ago. As children growing up across the straits from Ynys Seiriol, we were frequently regaled with the story of the close friendship of Seiriol and Cybi. Each morning they would journey six hours to meet each other at Clorach in the centre of Anglesey, before returning home in the afternoon. In the morning, Cybi would walk facing the sun in the east, with Seiriol walking with his back to the sun. In the afternoon, with the sun having travelled across the sky, Cybi would face sunshine again on his way home, while Seiriol would once again walk with his back to the sun. So, Cybi ended up with a tan that would put Donald Trump to shame, and Seiriol ended up pale as a ghost. Thus, their nicknames were sealed – Seiriol Wyn (Seiriol the White) and Cybi Felyn (Cybi the Yellow).

We found this tale rather amusing as children, not least because our experience in rainy Wales was that we rarely saw the sun! But, as I recalled this story during my walk, it struck me that it was not an apt metaphor for our journeys. The idea that the sun *always* shines on us or that we *always* walk in dark shadows did not reflect my experience of my pilgrimage. Alongside times of pain and hardship in the journey were wonderfully uplifting and joyous times, as well as times of profound revelation. After all, pilgrimages are a microcosm of the journey of life, and all our lives have ups and downs, highs and lows, joys and pains, and sunshine and shadows.

While I can now brag that I have walked the 140-mile Pilgrim's Way, it was actually Europe's most famous pilgrimage trail that I had most wanted to tread. The Camino de Santiago is a 500-mile journey starting in the south of France and finishing in Santiago de Compostela in north-west Spain. I was due to walk it with some friends after my North Wales walk. However, I was left broken-hearted to have to pull out of the trip due to my back injury. To cheer me up, one of my friends brought back a gift – a small, wooden Santiago pilgrim. Santiago is Spanish for St James, who, as well as being one of Jesus' twelve disciples, is the patron saint of travellers. The most striking thing about my little St James pilgrim, though, is the fact that half his face is dark and half his face is pale. While I recovered from my injury during my second pilgrimage, it was not Seiriol and Cybi I would contemplate on for reassurance and inspiration. Instead, it was my wooden Santiago ornament. Sometimes our lives are happy and joyous. But none of us

walk in the beautiful sunshine all the time. There are times even getting out of bed is a real struggle. And on the days during my recovery
when life was hard, whether I was feeling anxious, depressed or in
pain, I looked to my wooden St James to reassure myself that, while
I might be walking in the darkness of shadows, soon the sunshine
would break through.

The other striking fact about my little St James is that he is made from
driftwood. This discarded dead tree has been worn and battered by
sea and storms. It was then made by a skilled creator into something
beautiful, something that has been able to lift my heart during anxious
times. As such, my driftwood Santiago became an emblem to enlighten
and inspire me. As I gazed on it, it would remind me that, however
much we feel battered and broken by the storms of life and however
much we feel lost and discarded, God continues to work in us, creating
something that can still bring hope and joy to others. God does not
simply use our uplifting times in the beautiful sunshine to bring hope,
love and compassion to his broken world. He also uses the painful and
difficult times when we have languished in the dark shadows.

## Growing through the grind

In recent years, singer-songwriters have taken to writing songs for their
children. Pop songs such as Jason Mraz's 'Have it All', Jamie Lawson's
'When it Comes to Love' and Milow's 'Nice to Meet You' have uplifting
and moving lyrics that express a deep desire to keep children safe and
away from harm and suffering. In Mraz's multi-million-selling hit single,
for example, he wishes 'unquestionable' health, wealth and happiness
to his young child. The accompanying video is colourful, joyful and fun.

In the song 'Wish You Pain', though, the renowned singer-songwriter
Andy Grammer delivers a message to his young daughter that initially
seems shocking. Rather than wishing her only joy and happiness, he
prays for her to experience hardship and suffering. While this might
sound harsh or even cruel, Grammer explained in an interview that

his perspective comes from his own painful journey, including the tragic loss of his mother. Although every part of him wishes he had not endured that loss, he recognises it as a pivotal experience that shaped him into a more compassionate and empathetic person.

The accompanying music video brings the song's message into sharper focus. In it, Grammer invites fans to share the moments of pain that shaped their lives and to describe how those experiences changed them. As the song plays, we see fans speaking with Grammer, with their stories displayed as subtitles on the screen – tales of grief, illness, injury, addiction, infertility, unemployment and depression. Through their words, we see how they found growth and transformation in the midst of their struggles. Far from being a cruel wish, the song is, therefore, an expression of deep love. Grammer wants his daughter to grow into her fullest, most resilient self, who is shaped not just by joy but also by the strength and wisdom that come from facing life's challenges.

The song's insistence that pain aids our growth and is necessary for a loving and fulfilled life, echoes a theological theory known as 'the vale of soul-making'. This embraces 19th-century poet John Keats' phrase to summarise the belief that it is through pain and suffering that our souls grow and develop. It is held that courage, compassion, love and resilience are the result of the grind of our daily struggles. Christians should be highly suspicious of this as a standalone theory to explain the necessity of suffering. After all, it is dangerous to claim there is a need to suffer for personal development. Christians cannot hold that God desires us to experience trauma and affliction. Similarly, the theory fails to account for those whose suffering dehumanises and destroys them to such an extent that there is no opportunity for growth. Still, there is no denying that many people do grow through the storms of life and that adversity can help increase empathy, compassion and care for others who face trials and tribulations.

# Redeeming suffering

In a medieval Islamic tale, the wife of the philosopher Mullah Nasruddin is said to have found him searching the ground outside his house. He informed her he had lost his key. After assisting his search, she finally asked where he had dropped it. Nasruddin answered that he had lost it inside the house. 'So why on earth are you looking for it outside?', his perplexed wife asks. 'Because it's much lighter out here than inside', Nasruddin answers. Likewise, our contemporary world is inclined to look in ill-considered places for personal growth. Sometimes we are persuaded that our self-development is to be rooted in achievements and success. At other times, it is happiness, wealth or fame that are seen as the key to a fulfilled life. Yet my North Wales pilgrimage and my journey of recovery revealed the paradox that so many wise sages have taught – that personal growth is somehow found in our response to adversity. It is not *despite* the pain we feel and the suffering we endure that we are able to make a deeper contribution to the lives of those around us, but precisely *because* of the afflictions we journey through.

This, of course, is a concept that is very much rooted in the biblical witness. The Old Testament tells the story of a people who find their identity in the midst of hardship, whether through exodus, exile or foreign oppression. But it also brings us vivid and inspiring tales of individuals who rise above misfortune. From Abraham, Joseph and Moses to Ruth, Esther and Daniel, we see lives transformed by faith and resilience. In the New Testament, we encounter figures like the Virgin Mary and the apostle Paul, who trust deeply in a God who can bring good even from grief and hardship. Most powerfully, though, the New Testament itself is built around an overarching narrative of redeemed suffering. The cross stands as a profound reminder that God is present in the pain he never intended for us to endure, while the resurrection boldly proclaims that suffering will not have the final word.

And so Christians do not regard time in the shadows, with our backs to the sun, as time wasted. God is working in even our most arduous moments of struggle, reinterpreting pain and redeeming suffering.

When we emerge from the darkness, we not only grow more grateful for the sunlight we face but also develop a deeper empathy for those still dwelling in the shadowlands. In John's gospel, Jesus reminds us that seeds need to fall into the cold, dark soil to emerge into the light as a beautiful harvest (John 12:24). Not that all seeds thrive. Some seeds wither in the hard earth and there is no denying that life's struggles can wear us down or even break us. But paradoxically, for many, these same challenges lay the foundation for flourishing. They lead us to a deeper understanding of both ourselves and our role in the lives of others. Psychologist Richard Farson describes this as a 'calamity theory' of growth, where pivotal moments of crisis, though painful, redefine how we see ourselves and so catalyse personal transformation. The outcome of life's calamitous events is not predetermined. While some may sink into despair, others find in the rubble a path to profound growth, resilience and hope.

## Gifts that keep on taking

Slowly but surely, I began to recognise something profound in the struggles I was facing in my journey of recovery. Not that I would have chosen to go through turmoil and depression. Nor would I claim that something better came out of the situation. However, I was bearing witness to the incongruous truth that God is present in our suffering, continually acting in every situation to bring healing, goodness and redemption. As philosopher Thomas Jay Oord puts it: 'God squeezes something good out of the bad he didn't want in the first place.'

At the height of his career, British magician Dynamo was captivating millions worldwide with his awe-inspiring performances. Yet his meteoric rise came to a halt when he was struck by a relentless chronic illness following the removal of part of his intestine due to Crohn's disease. In the Sky TV series *Dynamo: Beyond Belief*, which chronicles his recovery, he poignantly asks: 'What if I could turn my disability into a superpower?' Similarly, actor Michael J. Fox refers to his battle with Parkinson's disease as 'a gift', though he candidly adds that it is 'a gift that keeps on taking'. Life's hardships come in many forms, whether illness, grief, anxiety, broken relationships or loss of livelihood. Yet, even in these dark moments, God's presence invites us to discover the paradoxical truth that there is an intimate connection between shadows and sunshine.

This is something our spiritual ancestors understood deeply. Interestingly, in Hebrew, at least two words for 'burden' (*maseth* and *yehabeka*) can also be translated as 'gift'. This dual meaning transforms the reading of a number of scriptural verses, including Psalm 55:22, which can be translated as: 'Cast your *gift* on the Lord and he will sustain you.'

Yet, for most of us, it is only with hindsight that we recognise that times of turmoil can be gifts to be received, rather than times to be endured. As we are journeying through the barren land of burden, the fact that we may one day view the struggle as part of our superpower is scant reassurance. As I lay in pain on my red sofa, well-meaning platitudes fell flat. I had no patience for clichés nor neatly packaged wisdom. What truly reached me in those moments of raw vulnerability was the quiet reassurance that, no matter how distant he seemed, God was walking alongside me. This simple yet profound truth resonated deeply. It was a reminder of the biblical promise of God's companionship. As such, it harkens back to the harmony of Eden, where God walked with humanity (Genesis 3:8; see also Leviticus 26:12), and points forward to the hope of a future paradise yet to come.

In her book *Wayfarer*, Phoebe Smith shares her own journey along the Pilgrim's Way, vividly capturing struggles that felt all too familiar to me. She writes of the frustration of losing her way, the torment of unquenchable thirst, and the relentless challenges posed by barbed wire, deep mud, and even confrontations with lively herds of cows. Reflecting on her experience, she offers a succinct and striking definition of pilgrimage: 'a walk defined by toughness and obstacles'. In reality, though, the physical dangers of the walk she details were not the real struggles of the pilgrimage. As she travelled, she mulled over both past and present hardships, which included grief, domestic violence, isolation, loneliness and prejudice. Looking back and facing the mess and misfortune of her life was the real challenge of her walk.

In much the same way, many of our journeys in life are marked by pain and struggle. Sometimes, our travels take a physical toll. Often, though, we face inner battles on our journeys, as thoughts and reflections weigh heavily on us. None of us are spared from the darker paths of life's pilgrimages. Yet, for the Christian, the call to cling to hope is clear, even when shadows threaten to obscure the way forward. As the actor Anna Deavere Smith writes, we need to become 'hopeaholics'.

## Keep moving forward

To champion hope in the face of adversity has been a lifetime journey for me. Fifteen years ago, I wrote a book that resonated with many, exploring the search for hope and meaning in our lives. But my journey as a writer began much earlier, when, as an insufferable 13-year-old wearing a long black coat and delighting in everything miserable and melancholic, I published my first piece. 'Penmaenmawr Mountain' was a short poem that appeared in a book by the county library. Typical of the teenage goth that I was, the poem was dark and depressing, dripping in pessimism, gloom and despair. In the composition, I look out at the mountain behind my childhood home and see the workmen quarrying for granite, ripping open the bowels of the earth and destroying the beautiful landscape:

> 'I lift up mine eyes unto the hills'.
> But all I see is an enormous black hole like a gaping wound.
> The buzzard circles like a vulture over a corpse.
> The mist hangs low as if the sky weeps for the death of a mountain.

This sombre poem concludes with the vibrant, lush foliage that once adorned the majestic peak being replaced by dust and shattered stones and the crucified Jesus declaring: 'It is finished.'

As I walked across that very mountain during my pilgrimage, the poem came to mind, and I reflected on the half-truth it told. After all, the poem fails to recognise the hope and joy that the mountain still offers. Its crucifixion was certainly not the end of the story. Down the millennia, the mountain had been at the mercy of changing climates and vicious weather, surviving volcanic activity, thick ice and even time submerged underwater. Then, in recent centuries, the capricious greed of industrial activity scarred the landscape. But, as I followed the mountain's old Roman road during my pilgrimage, I recognised that the peak's beauty was still very much intact. In fact, even some of the scars it bore had become part of its beauty and lay witness to its glorious resurrection.

At the halfway point of the Pilgrim's Way, standing amid the beauty and majesty of my hometown's mountain, I found the strength to press on. Exhausted, in pain and limping with my injured knee, I realised that hope, the kind we find in the wonder of nature, in the comfort of friendship and family, or in the quiet assurance of God's presence, gives us the courage to keep moving forward. It is this hope that sustains us, even when the path seems impassable and the future feels impossible. As we journey on, weathering the slings and arrows of outrageous fortune, we grow in empathy and compassion for others who carry their own heavy burdens on their travels. And, through it all, we take just one step at a time, sometimes in sunshine, sometimes in shadows, and we hold on to the hope that each one of those steps will be redeemed. Then, looking back, we will see the truth of Kierkegaard's words, which relate to all our journeys in life: 'If one just keeps on walking, everything will be all right.'

# Study guide

This concise study guide is designed to stimulate deeper reflection for individuals or to spark lively discussion in small groups. It can be used during Lent, Advent or any other time of year. If you are following it during Lent, the Prologue questions can be considered on Ash Wednesday, followed by the six chapters over the six weeks of Lent, then the Epilogue questions on Easter Sunday (or sometime during Easter week).

## Prologue

1   Have you ever been on a pilgrimage or walked part of a pilgrimage route? What was that experience like? Consider the highs and lows of your journey – what inspired you, what challenged you and how it shaped your faith.

2   Life itself is full of journeys – some joyful, some difficult, some unexpected. Think about a part of your life that is like a pilgrimage, whether in your faith, relationships, work or health. Where have you seen God at work along the way?

3   In the busyness of life, it is easy to rush through our journeys without recognising God's presence. How could you create space to slow down and be more aware of him? Consider practical ways to notice God in your daily life.

4   When have you felt closest to God – during moments of joy or in times of struggle? Or perhaps it is in the in-between times? Reflect on how we can become more aware of God's presence in every season of life, not just at the obvious times.

## For prayer

Pray that we open our eyes to God's presence in our journeys – through the people we meet, the places we visit and the moments we experience, whether joyful, challenging or quiet. May we recognise his kingdom at work in our life journeys, even in our busiest or most difficult moments.

# Chapter 1 Suffering

1   How difficult is it to trust God in the dark seasons of life? Have you ever had to lean on him during a time of suffering, uncertainty or loss? Consider your experience or a time when you have seen someone else hold on to faith in the midst of struggle.

2   Stress, illness and worry can sometimes feel overwhelming. Where can we find comfort or peace in our journeys through the wilderness? Is there anything that has helped you hold on to hope through challenging times?

3   Fear and regret can feel like heavy burdens. Have there been moments in your journeys when they have seemed overpowering? Consider how you worked through negative thinking and what helped you to move forward.

4   Has God ever felt distant or silent on your journey? How did that impact your faith? Consider the idea that prayer might include the whole range of human emotions, including anger, frustration and protest. How can the Bible help us when we feel this way? Are there particular stories, books or verses that might comfort and encourage us when we face adversity?

## For prayer

Pray for Christ's light to shine in the places where we still carry pain or struggle. Ask for his healing, peace and presence in our lives, especially at moments when we find it hardest to trust him. May we learn to lean on God in our journeys, knowing that he walks alongside us.

# Chapter 2 Wonder

1  How often do you pause to soak in the beauty of God's creation? Whether it is towering trees, delicate flowers, birdsong at dawn, the companionship of pets or even the simple joy of a houseplant, what part of the natural world inspires you most? Consider what lifts your spirit and helps you connect with God through creation.

2  The Bible calls us to care for God's creation, but what does that look like in your daily life? What practical steps can you take, big or small, to protect and nurture the world around us? Consider how you can live in a way that honours both God and the environment.

3  Many of us have a special place where we feel especially close to God. Where is that place for you? It could be somewhere in nature, a church, a quiet room or even a busy city street. What makes this place so meaningful, and how does it help you connect with God's presence?

4  God's wonder can touch us in all sorts of ways, through nature, music, friendships, stories, laughter or even in our seemingly mundane moments. Where do you most often experience a sense of awe and joy? Consider a time when something truly inspired you and made you aware of God's presence.

## For prayer

Pray that God opens our eyes to his wonder in every moment. Ask him to help us recognise his presence in creation and to be mindful of the beauty he has placed around us. Finally, pray that our hearts are stirred to care for all living things and to honour the world he has entrusted to us.

# Chapter 3 Signs

1   In what ways do you feel God communicates with you? Consider the ways you feel God speaks into your life, perhaps through scripture, prayer, other people or inner promptings. How do you make space to hear his voice amid the cacophony of daily life?

2   Have you ever experienced an unexpected coincidence that felt too meaningful to be random? Consider any moments of synchronicity in your life, times when you sensed God might be at work behind the scenes.

3   How do you discern what God's will is for your life? Is it ever possible to be completely certain? Discuss ways that you might recognise God's guidance and the potential challenges of trying to determine his will in your life.

4   Have you ever received what felt like a 'sign' from God? Consider a moment in your life when you felt God was leading you in a particular direction. How did he shape your choice or deepen your faith?

## For prayer

Pray for open hearts and minds to recognise the ways God speaks to us. Ask Jesus to guide us in discerning his will and to protect us from confusion or misunderstanding. Finally, spend a moment in silence, listening for God's still, small voice.

# Chapter 4 Company

1   How important is companionship in your life? Reflect on who among your friends and family has been there for you on your recent journeys in life, celebrating your highs and lifting you through the lows.

2   Is laughter really the best medicine? Consider when times of joy, humour or laughter have carried you through life's toughest moments. How can you stay open to God's gift of laughter and let it lift your heart, even in hard times?

3   Strangers can be angels in disguise, but do you really notice them? How easy is it to wear 'Christ-spectacles' and to recognise Jesus in the people you meet? Consider why many of us find this to be so challenging.

4   A beloved hymn declares: 'What a friend we have in Jesus.' But what does it really mean to call Jesus a 'friend'? Does that idea resonate with you? Reflect on how your friendship with Jesus shapes the way you connect with others in your daily life.

## For prayer

Ask God to help us cherish and nurture our relationships with friends and family. Pray for a heart that truly appreciates those who bring comfort, joy and hope into our lives. Finally, take a few quiet moments to rest in God's presence, allowing his Spirit to surround us in stillness.

# Chapter 5 Dependence

1  How easy is it for you to let go of the need to be in control? Consider some moments when fear or worry made it hard to trust that things would work out. Where was God in those times?

2  Reflect on the past 24 hours – how often did you rely on other people? You might want to consider food you have eaten, transport you have taken, places you gave visited and so on. How might recognising your dependence on others deepen your understanding of God's provision in your life?

3  What are you grateful for today? Reflect on how you can cultivate a daily 'attitude of gratitude' and become more aware of the blessings all around you.

4  How can you 'pay forward' the blessings and gifts of your life? Could you commit to carrying out some simple acts of kindness over the next few weeks?

## For prayer

Pray that we come to truly recognise the gifts God has placed in our lives and that we reflect his boundless generosity in the way we treat others. Ask God to open our eyes to the everyday moments where we can share his love, knowing that even the smallest acts of kindness can make a difference.

# Chapter 6 Hope

1  How easy is it to look beyond your own struggles to become a source of hope for others? Consider how simply being present and 'available' can be a gift to those around you.

2  Recall a moment of joy from your past. When was it? Who was with you? What happened? Reflect on how that memory can bring hope to your present and future.

3  Consider the idea that your scars, both physical and emotional, help shape who you are. In what ways have your own struggles been transformed into something that can be a gift to others? How has God redeemed those experiences, turning them into a testimony of hope?

4  Where do you find hope? Consider where you might find signs of new life and resurrection, both in your own life and in the world around you. How can recognising these moments strengthen your faith?

## For prayer

Pray for all those who are facing their own struggles, their own 'dark nights of the soul'. In a moment of silence, take time to consider those we personally know who are going through difficult times. Ask God to bring them comfort, strength and a renewed sense of hope.

# Epilogue

1  Take a moment to reflect on your life – your seasons of joy, as well as the more challenging times. How have these experiences shaped you? In what ways has God's love carried you through life's highs and lows, giving you strength and comfort?

2  Reflect on the struggles you have faced. Have they deepened your empathy and compassion? Consider whether life's storms refine you, making you more attuned to the pain of others. How can you use your own experiences to shine as beacons of hope in the darkness?

3   Consider the biblical stories of redeemed suffering, as people who journey in the wilderness emerge transformed. Which of these stories speaks to you most deeply? How does scripture reveal itself as a book of resurrection and hope?

4   As you look back on your journey through this book, what insights have resonated most with you? Which truths will you carry forward and which might inspire you to make changes in your own life?

## For prayer

Pray that God's presence transforms our journeys as we open the whole of our lives, the sunshine and the shadows, to his love. Ask that we are shaped into bearers of his promise of new life and that we become vessels of his light and hope.

# Bibliography

Many of the quotations I have used in this book have been collected over many years from films, books, newspapers, music lyrics, reliable internet sources and television programmes. However, to give readers the opportunity to explore topics further, I include here a bibliography of the texts that were used in the writing of the book.

David Abram, *The Spell of the Sensuous: Perception and language in a more-than-human world* (Vintage, 1997)

Aelred of Rievaulx, *Spiritual Friendship: The classic text with a spiritual commentary* (Ave Maria Press, 2008)

Khaled Anatolios, 'Divine Disponibilité: The hypostatic ethos of the Holy Spirit', *Pro Ecclesia*, 12:3 (2003)

Augustine, *The City of God* (Penguin Classics, 2003)

Augustine, *Confessions* (Penguin Classics, 2003)

Karl Barth, *Church Dogmatics Volume 2 Part 1: The doctrine of God* (T&T Clark International, 2003)

Richard Bauckham, *Gospel of Glory: Major themes in Johannine theology* (Baker Academic, 2015)

Bernard D. Beitman, *Connecting with Coincidence: The new science for using synchronicity and serendipity in your life* (Health Communications, 2016)

Nikolai Berdyaev, *The Divine and the Human* (Semantron Press, 2009)

Dietrich Bonhoeffer, *Sanctorum Communio: Dietrich Bonhoeffer Works, Volume 1* (Fortress Press, 2009)

Dietrich Bonhoeffer, *Life Together* (SCM, 2015)

David J. Bosch, *Transforming Mission: Paradigm shifts in theology of mission* (Orbis, 1991)

Brian Brock, *Wondrously Wounded: Theology, disability, and the body of Christ* (Baylor University Press, 2019)

Walter Brueggemann, *An Introduction to the Old Testament: The canon and Christian imagination* (Westminster John Knox Press, 2021)

Will Buckingham, *Hello, Stranger: Stories of connection in a divided world* (Granta, 2021)

John Bunyan, *The Pilgrim's Progress* (Penguin Classics, 2008)

Oliver Burkeman, *Four Thousand Weeks: Time management for mortals* (Vintage, 2022)

Joseph Campbell, *The Hero with A Thousand Faces* (New World Library, 2012)

Fritjof Capra, *The Web of Life: A new scientific understanding of living systems* (Anchor, 1997)

Clare Carlisle, *Philosopher of the Heart: The restless life of Søren Kierkegaard* (Penguin, 2020)

Geoffrey Chaucer, *The Canterbury Tales* (Penguin Classics, 2003)

Joan Chittister, *Between the Dark and the Daylight: Embracing the contradictions of life* (Image, 2015)

Kate Clanchy, *Some Kids I Taught and What They Taught Me* (Swift Press, 2022)

John Clare, *Major Works* (Oxford University Press, 2008)

Douglas Coupland, *Life after God* (Simon & Schuster, 2002)

Mihaly Csikszentmihalyi, *Flow: The psychology of optimal experience* (Harper Perennial, 2008)

Dante, *The Divine Comedy: Inferno, Purgatorio, Paradiso* (Penguin Classics, 2012)

Jacques Derrida, *Hospitality: Volume I* (University of Chicago Press, 2023)

Jacques Derrida, *Hospitality: Volume 2* (University of Chicago Press, 2024)

John Donne, *Selected Poems* (Penguin Classics, 2006)

Ian Dunt and Dorian Lynskey, *Conspiracy Theory: The story of an idea* (W&N, 2024)

Mary C. Earle, *Celtic Christian Spirituality: Essential writings* (SPCK, 2012)

Meister Eckhart, *Selected Writings* (Penguin Classics, 1994)

Edith Eger, *The Choice: Even in hell hope can flower* (Rider, 2018)

Mircea Eliade, *The Sacred and the Profane: The nature of religion* (Oxford University Press, 2012)

Elisabeth Elliot, *Suffering is Never for Nothing* (B&H, 2019)

Mark W. Elliott, *Providence: A biblical, historical, and theological account* (Baker Academic, 2020)

Albert Ellis, *Rational Emotive Behavior Therapy: A therapist's guide* (Impact, 2016)

Epicurus, 'Letter to Menoeceus' in *The Essential Epicurus* (Prometheus, 1993)

Bruce G. Epperly, *Process Theology: Embracing adventure with God* (Energion, 2014)

Joseph Epstein, *Friendship: An exposé* (Mariner, 2007)

Steve Farrar, *Manna: When you're out of options, God will provide* (Nelson, 2016)

Richard Farson and Ralph Keyes, *Whoever Makes the Most Mistakes Wins: The paradox of innovation* (Free Press, 2002)

Charles Foster, *The Sacred Journey* (Thomas Nelson, 2010)

Richard Foster, *Celebration of Discipline: The path to spiritual growth* (Hodder and Stoughton, 2008)

Richard J. Foster and James Bryan Smith (eds), *Devotional Classics: Selected Readings for Individuals and Groups* (Hodder and Stoughton, 1993)

Michael J. Fox, *Lucky Man* (Ebury, 2003)

Michael J. Fox, *No Time Like the Future: An optimist considers mortality* (Headline, 2020)

Viktor E. Frankl, *Man's Search for Meaning: The classic tribute to hope from the Holocaust* (Rider, 2004)

John Gillibrand, *Disabled Church – Disabled Society: The implications of autism for philosophy, theology and politics* (Jessica Kingsley, 2010)

Jane Goodall with Phillip Berman, *Reason for Hope: A spiritual journey* (Grand Central, 2004)

Jane Goodall and Douglas Abrams, *The Book of Hope: A survival guide for an endangered planet* (Viking, 2021)

James Goodman, *But Where Is the Lamb? Imagining the story of Abraham and Isaac* (Schocken Books, 2013)

Niall Griffiths, *Grits* (Vintage, 2001)

Elfed Gruffydd, *Llŷn* (Gwasg Carreg Gwalch, 2003)

Stanley Hauerwas, 'To be befriended: a meditation on friendship and the disabled', *Church Life Journal: A journal for the McGrath Institute for Church Life* (November 2019)

Gary Hayden, *Walking with Plato: A philosophical hike through the British Isles* (Oneworld, 2017)

Anne Hayward, *A Pilgrimage around Wales: In search of a significant conversation* (Y Lolfa, 2018)

Julian Heath, *Ancient Echoes: The early history of a Welsh Peninsula* (Gwasg Carreg Gwalch, 2006)

Martin Heidegger, *Being and Time* (State University of New York Press, 2010)

George Herbert, *The Complete English Poems* (Penguin Classics, 1992)

Thomas Hobbes, *Leviathan* (Penguin Classics, 2017)

A.E. Housman, *A Shropshire Lad and Other Poems* (Penguin Classics, 2010)

Gerard W. Hughes, *God of Surprises* (Darton, Longman and Todd, 1990)

Robert Hughes, *The Shock of the New: Art and the century of change* (Thames and Hudson, 1991)

Trystan Owain Hughes, *Finding Hope and Meaning in Suffering* (SPCK, 2010)

Drew Hunter, *Made for Friendship: The relationship that halves our sorrows and doubles our joys* (Crossway, 2018)

Lewis Hyde, *The Gift: How the creative spirit transforms the world* (Canongate, 2007)

Haley Goranson Jacob, *Conformed to the Image of His Son: Reconsidering Paul's theology of glory in Romans* (IVP Academic, 2018)

William James, *The Varieties of Religious Experience: A study in human nature* (Penguin Classics, 1985)

*The Jewish Study Bible* (Oxford University Press, 2014)

John of the Cross, *Dark Night of the Soul* (Dover, 2003)

Andrew Jones, *Pilgrimage: The journey to remembering our story* (BRF Ministries, 2011)

Julian of Norwich, *Revelations of Divine Love* (DS Brewer, 1998)

Carl Jung, *Memories, Dreams, Reflections* (Fontana, 1986)

Carl Jung and Wolfgang Pauli, *The Interpretation of Nature and the Psyche* (Ishi Press, 2012)

Erling Kagge, *Philosophy for Polar Explorers* (Viking, 2019)

Erling Kagge, *Walking: One step at a time* (Viking, 2019)

Paul Kammerer, *The Law of Seriality: A theory of recurrences in daily life and world events* (Jason David Bulkeley, 2024)

Timothy Keller, *The Timothy Keller Sermon Archive* (Redeemer Presbyterian Church, 2013)

Margery Kempe, *The Book of Margery Kempe* (Penguin Classics, 1985)

Søren Kierkegaard, *Fear and Trembling* (Penguin, 1985)

Søren Kierkegaard, *Concluding Unscientific Postscript to Philosophical Fragments* (Princeton University Press, 1992)

Brian Klaas, *Fluke: Chance, chaos, and why everything we do matters* (John Murray, 2025)

Karl-Josef Kuschel, *Laughter: A theological reflection* (SCM, 1994)

Belden C. Lane, *Landscapes of the Sacred: Geography and narrative in American spirituality* (Johns Hopkins University Press, 2001)

Belden C. Lane, *The Great Conversation: Nature and the care of the soul* (Oxford University Press, 2019)

William Large, *Levinas' Totality and Infinity: A reader's guide* (Bloomsbury Academic, 2015)

Peter J. Leithart, *Traces of the Trinity: Signs of God in creation and human experience* (Brazos, 2015)

Emmanuel Levinas, *Time and the Other* (Duquesne University Press, 1987)

C.S. Lewis, *The Four Loves* (William Collins, 1960)

C.S. Lewis, *The Problem of Pain* (Fount, 2002)

C.S. Lewis, *Surprised by Joy* (Collins, 2012)

C.S. Lewis, *The Horse and His Boy* (Harper Collins, 2015)

C.S. Lewis, *The Lion, the Witch, and the Wardrobe* (Harper Collins, 2015)

C.S. Lewis, *Prince Caspian* (Harper Collins, 2015)

Dorian Llywelyn, *Sacred Place, Chosen People: Land and national identity in Welsh spirituality* (University of Wales Press, 1999)

Richard Louv, *Last Child in the Woods: Saving our children from nature-deficit disorder* (Atlantic, 2010)

Martin Luther, *Lectures on Romans* (Westminster John Knox Press, 1961)

Martin Luther, *The Freedom of a Christian* (Crossway, 2023)

David McCord, *What Cheer: An anthology of American and British humorous and witty verse* (The Modern Library, 1955)

Gabriel Marcel, *Homo Viator: Introduction to the metaphysic of hope* (St Augustine's Press, 2010)

Gabriel Marcel, *The Mystery of Being* (Legare Street Press, 2023)

Karl Marx, *Economic and Philosophical Manuscripts of 1844* (Prometheus, 1988)

Marcel Mauss, *The Gift* (HAU, 2016)

Nick Mayhew-Smith, *The Naked Hermit: A journey to the heart of Celtic Britain* (SPCK, 2019)

Donella H. Meadows, *Thinking in Systems: A primer* (Chelsea Green Publishing, 2017)

Ann Memmott, 'Welcoming autistic people in our churches and communities', Diocese of Oxford, 2015

Maurice Merleau-Ponty, *The World of Perception* (Routledge, 2004)

Emma Mitchell, *The Wild Remedy: How nature mends us* (Michael O'Mara, 2019)

Jürgen Moltmann, *The Crucified God* (SCM, 1974)

Jürgen Moltmann, *The Church in the Power of the Spirit* (SCM, 1992)

Maud Monahan, *Life and Letters of Janet Erskine Stuart: Superior General of the Society of the Sacred Heart 1857 to 1914* (Forgotten Books, 2019)

John I. Morgans and Peter C. Noble, *Our Holy Ground: The Welsh Christian experience* (Y Lolfa, 2016)

Iris Murdoch, *The Sovereignty of Good* (Routledge, 2010)

Thomas Nagel, *Mind and Cosmos: Why the materialist Neo-Darwinian conception of nature is almost certainly false* (Oxford University Press, 2012)

Jean Napier, *Bardsey: Now and then* (Gwasg Carreg Gwalch, 2018)

Wallace J. Nichols, *Blue Mind: How water makes you happier, more connected and better at what you do* (Abacus, 2018)

John O'Donohue, *Anam Cara: Spiritual wisdom from the Celtic world* (Bantam, 1999)

Elizabeth Oldfield, *Fully Alive: Tending to the soul in turbulent times* (Hodder and Stoughton, 2024)

Thomas Jay Oord, *God Can't: How to believe in God and love after tragedy, abuse, and other evils* (SacraSage Press, 2019)

Graham Panes, *Voyages of the Celtic Saints* (Gwasg Carreg Gwalch, 2017)

Plato, *The Republic* (Penguin Classics, 2007)

Martin Plimmer and Brian King, *Beyond Coincidence: Stories of amazing coincidences and the mystery and mathematics that lie behind them* (Icon, 2019)

Stephen G. Post, *God and Love on Route 80: The hidden mystery of human connectedness* (Mango, 2019)

Sunita Puri, *That Good Night: Life and medicine in the eleventh hour* (Constable, 2019)

Richard Rice, *Suffering and the Search for Meaning: Contemporary responses to the problem of pain* (IVP Academic, 2014)

David Richo, *The Power of Coincidence: How life shows us what we need to know* (Shambhala, 2007)

Michael Rosen and Helen Oxenbury, *We're Going on a Bear Hunt* (Walker Books, 1993)

Squire Rushnell, *When God Winks: How the power of coincidence guides your life* (Howard, 2018)

Oliver Sacks, *Gratitude* (Picador, 2015)

Michael J. Sandel, *The Tyranny of Merit: What's become of the common good?* (Penguin, 2021)

Gary E. Schwartz, *The G.O.D. Experiments: How science is discovering God in everything, including us* (Atria, 2007)

Rupert Sheldrake, *The Presence of the Past: Morphic residence and the habits of nature* (Icon, 2011)

Rupert Sheldrake, *Science and Spiritual Practices* (Coronet, 2017)

Peter Sills, *Light in the Darkness: Exploring the Path of Christian Hope* (Sacristy, 2020)

Suzanne Simard, *Finding the Mother Tree: Uncovering the Wisdom and Intelligence of the Forest* (Penguin, 2022)

Georg Simmel, *On Individuality and Social Forms*, edited by Donald
   N. Levine (University of Chicago Press, 1971)
James Bryan Smith, *Room of Marvels: A story about heaven that
   heals the heart* (IVP, 2020)
Phoebe Smith, *Wayfarer: Love, loss and life on Britain's ancient paths*
   (HarperNorth, 2024)
Dorothee Soelle, *Suffering* (Darton, Longman and Todd, 1975)
Aleksandr Solzhenitsyn, *The Gulag Archipelago 1918–1956* (Harper
   Perennial, 2007)
Susan Sontag, *Illness as Metaphor; AIDS and its Metaphors* (Penguin,
   2009)
Peter Stanford, *The Extra Mile: A 21st century pilgrimage*
   (Continuum, 2011)
Galen Strawson, *Consciousness and its Place in Nature: Why
   physicalism entails panpsychism* (Imprint Academic, 2006)
John Swinton, *Becoming Friends of Time: Disability, timefullness,
   and gentle discipleship* (SCM Press, 2017)
Martyn Symington, *Sacred Britain: A guide to places that stir the soul*
   (Bradt, 2011)
David Tacey, *How to Read Jung* (Granta, 2006)
Donna Tartt, *The Goldfinch* (Abacus, 2014)
Barbara Brown Taylor, *God and Pain: The mystery of suffering*
   (Canterbury Press, 2018)
Charles Taylor, *A Secular Age* (Belknap Press, 2018)
R.S. Thomas, *Counterpoint* (Bloodaxe Books, 1990)
R.S. Thomas, *Mass for Hard Times* (Bloodaxe Books, 1992)
R.S. Thomas, *Collected Poems: 1945–1990* (W&N, 2000)
J.R.R. Tolkien, *The Silmarillion* (HarperCollins, 2013)
J.R.R. Tolkien, *The Lord of the Rings: The Two Towers* (HarperCollins,
   2022)
Leo Tolstoy, *War and Peace* (Penguin Classics, 2007)
Graham Tomlin, *Why Being Yourself Is a Bad Idea: And other
   countercultural notions* (SPCK, 2020)
Ivan Turgenev, *The Diary of a Superfluous Man and Other Novellas*
   (Alma Classics, 2019)

Graham B. Usher, *Places of Enchantment: Meeting God in landscapes* (SPCK, 2012)

Iyanla Vanzant, *Trust: Mastering the four essential trusts* (Hay House, 2017)

Miroslav Volf, *Free of Charge: Giving and forgiving in a culture stripped of grace* (Zondervan, 2005)

*The Way of a Pilgrim and The Pilgrim Continues His Way* (Image, 2003)

Sally Welch, *Pilgrim Journeys: Pilgrimages for walkers and armchair travellers* (BRF, 2017)

J.E. Caerwyn Williams, Peredur I. Lynch, and R. Geraint Gruffydd (eds), *Gwaith Meilyr Brydydd a'i Ddisgynyddion* (University of Wales Press, 1994)

Rowan Williams, *Tokens of Trust: An introduction to Christian belief* (Canterbury Press, 2007)

Rowan Williams, *Open to Judgement: Sermons and addresses* (Darton, Longman and Todd, 2014)

Edward O. Wilson, *Biophilia: The human bond with other species* (Harvard University Press, 1990)

Peter Wohlleben, T*he Hidden Life of Trees: What they feel, how they communicate – discoveries from a secret world* (William Collins, 2017)

William Wordsworth, *Collected Poems* (Penguin Classics, 2004)

N.T. Wright, *Evil and the Justice of God* (SPCK, 2006)

Philip Yancey, *Where Is God When It Hurts?* (Marshall Pickering, 2002)

**BRF** Ministries

*Inspiring people of all ages to grow in Christian faith*

BRF Ministries is the home of Anna Chaplaincy, BRF Resources, Messy Church and Parenting for Faith

As a charity, our work would not be possible without fundraising and gifts in wills.
To find out more and to donate,
visit brf.org.uk/give or call +44 (0)1235 462305

Registered with
FUNDRAISING
**REGULATOR**

www.ingramcontent.com/pod-product-compliance
Lightning Source LLC
LaVergne TN
LVHW051410080426
835508LV00022B/3025